UNDERWEAR

The Fashion History

ALISON CARTER

DRAMA BOOK PUBLISHERS
New York

First published 1992

© Alison Carter 1992

Typeset by
Goodfellow & Egan Phototypesetting Ltd, Cambridge
and printed in Hong Kong

Drama Book Publishers
260 Fifth Avenue
New York
New York 10001

ISBN 0-89676-120-7

Contents

Acknowledgements

Mr Negley Harte and The Pasold Research Fund provided a generous travel grant to assist my research into underwear in museum collections. I would like to thank my editor at Batsford, Pauline Snelson, for all her hard work and patience, and Aileen Ribeiro, my former tutor at the Courtauld Institute of Art, for encouraging me to take on the subject.

A number of corsetry and underwear companies have assisted my enquiries. I would particularly like to thank Sarah Bennett at Berlei, Brettles, Contessa, Damart, Du Pont, Jeremy Lang at Chilprufe, Keith Ascough at Gossard, Meridian, La Perla, Jennifer Jones at Siegel and Stockman, Villia Wydryk and Louise Minifie at Layal, and Sue Loder at Triumph.

For personal interviews and assistance with reference to the Portsmouth Corset Industry, my thanks are extended to Kay Ainsworth (Charles Bayer), Doreen Ball (Twilfit), Councillor George Byng (Vollers), Mr Byrde (Twilfit), Mr Perrin (Twilfit), and Derek Voller (Vollers).

Museum staff were generous with time and assistance. I would especially like to thank the following: At Bath Museums Service, Penelope Byrde, Myra Mines and Andrea Parkes; at Brighton Museum, Shelley Tobin; at Cheltenham, Helen Brown; at Chertsey, Jane Sedge; at Leicester, Philip Warren; at Letchworth First Garden City Heritage Museum, Bob Lancaster; at Maidstone, Veronica Tonge; at Platt Hall, Manchester, Anthea Jarvis and Miles Lambert; at the Museum of London, Kay Staniland and Jill Spanner; at the Laing Art Gallery, Newcastle-upon-Tyne, Caroline Imlah; at Reading, Susan Read; at Salisbury, Susan Hartley; at Stoke-on-Trent, Jane Arthur and Liz Salmon, and at Worthing, Ann Wise.

Thanks to all who corresponded over photographs, in museums, pictures archives, and companies. Thanks also to the encouragement of friends, collectors, and curators, especially Silvia Druitt, Ian Edelman, Caroline Goldthorpe, Rosemary Hawthorne, Pam Inder, Margaret Macfarlane, the Mactaggarts, Linda Newington, Clare Rose, Margaret Smith, Madge Still, and Sue Welsh.

Hampshire County Museum Service allowed me to research the collections and have photographs taken. I owe a huge debt of gratitude to Trevor Evans, museum photographer, for his patience and professionalism. Peter Read kindly undertook additional photography.

Marion Davis in *The Gay Nineties*, 1930. This period farce ridiculed the fashions of the 1890s. Shown here, an elaborate be-ribboned corset.

Special thanks to my mother Sheila, for saving all those Daily Telegraph fashion pages, my father Alan, and brother Nigel, for moral support, and my fiancé Chung Tai, for providing the car, camera, computer, cups of coffee, excellent meals, and the moral support which made this book possible (sorry about all the (clean) underwear lying around!).

The Author and Publishers would also like to thank Celia McInnes for her contribution to the later chapters and Jacqui Lewis for assistance with research.

The Author and publishers would like to thank the following for permission to use pictures on the pages indicated below:
Albright-Knox Art Gallery, Buffalo, New York. Gift of William M. Chase, 1909, 47; Berlei, 132, 136a, 136b, 136c; City of Birmingham Museums and Art Galleries, 27b; Bridgeman Art Library, 15; British Film Institute, 6, 7, 80, 93, 108, 112, 114, 115, 146; Camera Press Ltd, 110, 117, 119, 124, 131, 133, 135; Colonial Williamsburg, USA, 25a, 25b; Costume Museum, Bath, 55; The Courtauld Institute, 17, 42, 43; Damart, 142; English Heritage, 19; E.T. Archive, 44a, 44b; Gossard, 82, 89, 103, 109, 133; HCMS, 2, 8a, 8b, 24a, 24b, 28a, 29, 35, 38a, 38b, 38c, 39, 46a, 46b, 46c, 52, 53, 54a, 54b, 87; Hulton Picture Collection, 13, 59; Imperial War Museum, 109; Kunsthaus, Zurich, 77, 86; Layal 135; Marks & Spencer, 111a, 111b, 111c, 122; Mary Evans Picture Library, 67, 70, 91, 96, 103, 113; Museum of London, 73; National Film Archive, 92; National Gallery, London, 21, 22; National Gallery, Prague, 79; National Portrait Gallery, London, 18a; Nelson-Atkins Museum of Art, Missouri, 27a; Platt Hall Museum, Manchester, 66a, 66b; Museo del Prado, Madrid, 16b; Rex Features, 116, 134; Spirella Archive, 81a, 81b; Tate Gallery, 50, 74; Triumph, 10, 11, 125, 129, 137, 138, 139, 142, 148, 149; Victoria & Albert Museum, 16a, 31, 33; Vintage Magazine Company, 70, 99a, 99b, 107, 147; Wallace Collection, 14, 26, 28b; Woburn Abbey. 18.

The pictures on pages 9, 30, 36, 37, 41, 48a, 48b, 49a, 49b, 52, 56, 57, 60, 61, 62, 65a, 65b, 68, 69, 71, 72, 73, 75, 78a, 78b, 76, 84, 85, 88, 89, 90, 91, 94a, 94b, 94c, 96, 97, 98a, 98b, 100, 101a, 101b, 102, 104, 106a, 106b, 108, 110, 112, 140, 141, 145a, 145b, 146, 149 were supplied by the author.

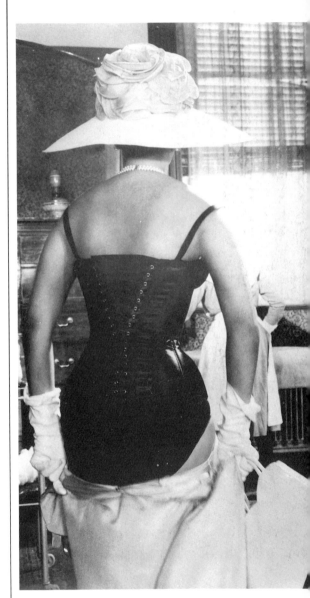

Sophia Loren in *The Millionairess*, 1960. A formidable leather corset, worn with panache.

L'Embarras du Choix, engraving c1860. Crossing a Stile. The lady wears a large frame-supported skirt and petticoat.

Matrimony, engraving, c1830. She wears a high waisted dress, allowing glimpses of petticoat, modesty piece or chemisette. He may be wearing a corset to give a very narrow waist.

Introduction

'Disgraceful I know but I can't help choosing my underwear with a view to it being seen!'[1]

Barbara Pym 1934

Whether it's the daring of revealing a decorated petticoat hem under a be-crinolined skirt, or a fear of falling under a tram, bus, or car and being rushed to hospital in unclean undies, women over the last 150 years have tended to consider the possible sight rather than the hidden aspect of underwear, a fact which has led to ornate design and embellishment far beyond the practicalities of the function of our nether garments, and equally, a degree of whiteness, or crisp fresh appearance, beyond the strictly necessary. Of course, there have been those who would have curled up in shame had their underwear ever been revealed in public, whether unsightly corsets or woolly vests. Both aspects are considered here – the covert display as well as the prudish covering-up of underwear – from 1840 up to the present day.

Modesty or Vanity?

Barbara Pym's comment reveals the 'naughty but nice' attitude to underclothes which many women share today, and judging from the lavish and intricate detail on surviving examples since the Victorian era, this is an attitude which has secretly prevailed throughout, amongst those wealthy enough to afford such luxuries. While men have been seduced by the sight of sexy underwear 'fleshed out', women have themselves been seduced by the touch of the lingerie fabrics, and have enjoyed wearing them next to the skin. The glamour of lingerie advertisements for at least a century has consistently struck a chord with women's hidden desires for sensuous and luxurious materials which would improve both their self-image, and their perceived appeal to the opposite sex.

The history of underwear is, however, about much more than just filmy lingerie. It begins as the story of the creation of a second skin, for modesty and comfort, and develops into the quest for a second skeleton, often alien to the natural form, which yet promotes the fashionable ideal. This ideal usually seems to have been regarded with suspicion by the majority at first, yet once adopted and familiar there has been a general reluctance to give it up.

This book looks at underwear in general from 1490, and in some depth over the last 150 years, highlighting women's underwear, which is perhaps the most intriguing, certainly the most variable. Reference to men's and children's is mainly limited to brief notes on specific innovations, particularly those with a bearing on developments in women's underwear. Stockings and tights are only briefly mentioned as they do not quite qualify as under (i.e. hidden) garments. For each of three 50-year periods, from 1840 to 1990, the book looks at the image 'outside in' – that is, the fashionable silhouette, and what layers were needed beneath to sustain this; then at the reality, 'inside out' – with an analysis of the actual clothes, fabrics, design and decoration; and finally at the context, 'round about' which focuses on reminiscences of wearing, and developments in the industry. These last sections also give details about making, cleaning and mending, together with notes on buying and selling.

Outside In

The aim of the 'Outside In' sections is to look at the outer clothes and the various layers which would have been worn beneath. It is very often possible to deduce, with some background knowledge, how many and what types and styles of undergarments are likely to have been worn. Changes in the fashionable silhouette are significant throughout. Developments in main garment fashions, most noticeably at necklines and waistlines, together with sleeve styles and lengths of hems, are key indicators to changes which will necessarily permeate down to the underlayers.

Mary Quant once lamented that the best underwear is essentially plain: 'I know I am always seduced myself by the prettiest, frilliest, laciest bras that look so good when you're half undressed. But under a dress, they are nothing but unsightly lumps and bumps'.[2] Sometimes the lumps and bumps give away under-

Photographic postcard c1910-12. Lady in high-waisted hobble skirt, with outrageous bondage feature at the knees. Practicality overruled by the dictates of fashion.

Men's combinations, 1992. This up-to-date cotton/Lycra bodysuit is the ultimate in uncomplicated and practical dressing.

cover secrets. For example, in mid-Victorian photographs, details may be observed such as the tell-tale ridges where crinoline frames reached only two-thirds of the way to the ground, or fabric fullness on upper arms where chemise sleeves were worn, or creasing of fabric over the ridges of corsets.

A Second Skin

Even when fashion has been at its most revolutionary, under-wear fashions may be said to have been evolutionary, and generally more practical than outer garments, having certain functions to fulfil. It is important to make a clear distinction between 'linen' and 'structural' underwear. The original linen or early 'lingerie' (often fine cotton or silk) undergarments worn next to the skin acted as a decent covering for the naked body, and as a temperature moderator, keeping the body comfortably warm or cool as required. They also provided a hygienic layer between the skin and the main, visible garments, at a time when daily baths were not taken, protecting the difficult-to-clean overgarments from dirt and odours, as well as shielding the skin from discomfort. 'Linen' undergarments have included shirts and chemises, camisoles and vests, drawers and knickers, com-binations and petticoats. Petticoats have on occasions crossed the boundaries between underwear and outerwear, becoming partially visible, showing at hem or at centre front, acting as foils for diaphanous outer garments. Sometimes they have also played a considerable supporting role, widening skirts and kicking out their hems.

A Second Skeleton

Those 'structural' undergarments which traditionally formed the second skeleton, performed one of two functions, either restricting or enlarging the natural contours of the human figure, and thus providing the basic shape for the fashionable dress of the period. An outer bone structure was quite literally achieved. Corsets moulded and displaced flesh, frames extended the silhouette, both using whalebone or later substitutes such as steel. Together they 'improved' the natural form, especially at bust, waist and hips. 'Structural' undergarments have included crinolines, bustles, bottom and bosom pads, brassieres, corse-lettes and girdles.

There have been identifiable fashion revivals of certain types of structural undergarments, particularly of expansive artificial skirt supports, from the farthingale to the mini-crini, and of restrictive corseting, whether formed with whalebone, plastic, or Lycra. We must ask why such variations on the same themes have been so popular when they have also been so impractical or uncomfortable, and so lampooned in the press. All manner of reasons may be suggested: dissatisfaction with the human form, playing up to men's fantasies of the ideal image by emphasizing erogenous zones, conspicuous consumption through the extravagant use of materials and sophisticated technology, or a desire to conform. The answers probably lie in a complex blending of these and other more practical reasons of stature and support, coupled with the impetus for all fashion's vagaries: desire for change.

Inside Out

The 'Inside Out' sections take a look at accidents of survival and documentary evidence to draw out key characteristics of each period including a survey of available materials and trimmings, the cut of named garments, and how different named garments developed one out of another.

Most often, when an undergarment was introduced it was substantial, and the term reflected this. As the garment evolved, it changed in character, often becoming smaller in some way, and diminutive terms were substituted, hence the changes from crinoline to crinolette, and from corset to corselette. Terms for men's outer leggings such as pantaloons and knickerbockers were shortened to pantees and knickers, when applied to the less capacious female undergarments. There have also been affectionate diminutive nicknames in each period, such as the 'undies', 'combies' and 'nighties' familiar to women around 1914.

Although brevity triumphed in the skimpy underwear of the 1960s and 1970s, it was flanked by substantial foundation garments and body fashions in the 1950s and 1980s respectively. Reduced weight has certainly been a factor in the development of modern corsetry and underwear. Spandex and more particularly Lycra, which has up to three times more restraining power than elastic for one third less weight, have largely cut out the need for boning. Fine silks from China and knitted merino wool and silk milanese, artificial fibres such as

'Noblesse' bodyshaper, 1990. Simplicity is the key with this pure white stretch lace and tricot bodyshaper.

11

rayon, and man-made fibres such as nylon and polyester are generally much lighter than those heavy linens, cottons and flannels of the nineteenth century. Shorter lengths and less fussy designs in mainstream fashions have necessitated less material for underwear, while starch, and heavy fastenings such as brass hooks and latterly zips have all been rendered unnecessary.

Underwear as Outerwear

There has of course been a continual redefining of the lines between linen and structural layers, and between underwear and outerwear. Lines have been especially fluid since the introduction of stretch fabrics such as knitted wool and silk, elastic, Spandex and Lycra. Lycra in particular has been combined, for 30 years, with a range of fibres to create snug-fitting, controlling underwear. Today it is available in a vast range and we may now see a single layer Lycra-based corsetry-cum-lingerie garment being worn next to the skin, and sometimes as outerwear by the more daring.

Already in the nineteenth century, some 'structural' undergarments had found their way to the surface in certain fashion quirks, notably with corset shapes on top in the 1820s, again in the 1870s with the 'cuirass' bodice, and in a boned cummerbund in the 1880s. In the 1910s, embroidered camisoles were designed to show through sheer blouses. The 1980s saw the Edwardian ribbon corset revived by followers of the pop star Madonna, who promoted a fashion for wearing all kinds of corsetry, including suspender belts, on top. Designers like Jean-Paul Gaultier transposed underwear designs like the whirlpool spirals from 1950s' bras onto upper fashions. Underwear fashions for the 1990s are currently following small exclusive lingerie companies like Janet Reger and Layal, who have designed deliciously embroidered and belaced silk and satin lingerie, which may be worn below as intimate apparel, or on top as evening wear.

Round About

These sections consider the social context of underwear, what it was like to wear, how it was washed, who made it and where. They look at the industry, charting the rise of a highly organized and sophisticated infrastructure which has perpetuated the whole concept of underwear. The success of advertising which has played a key role is also examined.

Each era has had its own conception of what is socially and morally acceptable, in terms of types of garments, terminology, and methods of advertising. The cover-up prudery of the Victorians was flanked by the more revealing eras of the French Revolution and the 'show-a-leg' 1920s. Terminology used has reflected the period with explicit terms such as 'bum rolls' and 'bosom friends' to the use of euphemisms such as 'unmentionables' and 'smalls'. Companies have found that updating terminology has helped to improve and sustain a forward image. Styles of advertising have become more direct, from the discreet use of dressing room scenes in 1830s fashion plates, to the use of live models in photographs of the 1920s, and models in underwear photographed outside in public places in the last 21 years.

Health concerns have been an issue for a century. Recently, new concerns have emerged about the environment. With the seduction of the new, and the range of different styles for different uses, day, evening, sport, maternity and nursing, protective, and different climates, we have a proliferation of undergarments in every closet, many hardly worn. New arguments are arising, questions are being asked about the long-term availability of traditional raw materials from animals, crops, and mineral sources. Even the most perennial of natural underwear fibres, cotton, has been chemically treated to a high degree in modern times: chlorine-bleached, with formaldehyde used in the finishing. Synthetics such as nylon and polyester are dependent on oil. The rich dark prints are wasteful on dye colour. Hence back-to-nature underwear is being promoted in environmentally-conscious firms: unbleached, undyed cotton boxer shorts and briefs which even come in recycled packaging!

With its glossary and list of companies, and notes on where surviving examples may be seen, this book provides points for further investigation but can only scratch the surface in pulling together the fashion history of underwear with the social and industrial history which underlies its every development.

The story of underwear is an undercover story whose exploration requires a certain detective instinct and a sense of the ridiculous. This book is written with the conviction that historic underwear in all its forms, should be appreciated and understood, and used to explain what our grandmothers would not tell us.

The Caterpillar Ride, 1938. Getting carried away at the funfair, a glimpse of suspenders and knickers.

— 1 —
1490–1690

General histories of European undergarments often look back 3,000 years, to illustrations of Cretan rush hoops from 2000 BC and Cretan lacing showing naked breasts thrust upwards, which are said to show the first hoops and corsets respectively.[1] A fourth-century Italian mosaic is then quoted as evidence for the first strapless bra with briefs.[2] Whatever the validity of particular attributions, such references point up two long-standing traditions – embellishment and distortion of the human form, and covering of delicate, vital organs.

Body Protection and the Concept of Modesty

A covering for the genitals, following on from biblical references to the fig-leaf and girded loins, certainly seems to be the obvious starting point for the development of underclothes. The first materials available were animal skins, and then early forms of woven cloth. By the Middle Ages, men had drawers in the form of a simple loincloth, a piece of fabric passed through the legs gathering up the genitals and tied around the hips with a lace; or alternatively, draped and baggy Saxon 'braies' of variable length ingeniously knotted and girdled. Sometimes these crossed the border into outerwear, and were called 'breeches'.

The Second Skin
There is scant evidence for female drawers being widely worn in Europe before the nineteenth century. Modesty for women was preserved by a long, loose robe, the female smock, which was paralleled by the nascent male shirt. The idea of a basic body-covering garment was not new. It had already appeared in a number of earlier forms, for instance in Egyptian Coptic and Islamic linen robes of the fourth to the twelfth centuries.

In cut, the shirt and smock were formed in a simple T-shape based on a rectilinear form of loom-woven cloth, seamed at the sides, with square sleeves set in, and under-arm gussets. While Coptic shirts incorporated bands of tapestry-woven decoration, suggesting that they were visible at least in part, the medieval undergarment was plain, without decoration.

Upper Classes

The perceived need for underclothing as distinct from main garments amongst the nobility seems to have become more acute when very finely woven outer garments were developed in the Middle Ages. An additional layer of warmth was welcomed and offered protection for the gown worn over, keeping it clean by providing a buffer from body heat and moisture. Odours and dirt could regularly be washed away from the undergarment, thus preventing soiling of expensive outer layers. At the same time, the skin was protected from the irritation of woollen fibres and fur linings, or the abrasiveness of a silk fabric woven with a metal thread (brocade). Cold to the touch, the linen could be warmed by the fire before wearing. Conversely, on a sunny day, white linen reflected the heat from the sun and cooled the body, making heavy outdoor work more tolerable.

Surviving examples of shirts and smocks, dating from about 1540, are from the upper classes. They are made of the finest linens: cambric, from Cambrai in Flanders, holland, originally from Holland, and lawn, delicate and diaphanous linen. Status may be inferred from the quality of material and cut, together with the degree of trimming and elaboration. In contrast, canvas was used for hardwearing shirts, made of locally grown hemp. Very coarse hemp-hair shirts were worn for heavy-duty work by labourers in the field. Such was the value of all cloth that hemp-hair shirts were considered precious enough to bequeath, amongst the poorer classes.

Shirts for Men

Being loose-fitting, the shirt or smock was slipped on over the head, with a slit to the centre front neckline as necessary. Men's shirts were seamed only to the waist, then left open to the knee for ease of movement. From around 1490, frills on neckline and cuffs were gradually exposed, and decorated with more extensive embroidery. The neckline was low on the collarbone at the

Saint Roch, *c*1480, attributed to Carlo Crivelli. A close up of a man's loincloth tied with a lace. Note also the ties on the hose, which would have been attached to the doublet.

Primavera, *c*1478, detail: The Three Graces, Sandro Botticelli. Only mythological figures could be shown semi-naked. The diaphanous draperies may be half-fantasy, but the detail of spherical collar buttons and gold loops suggest observation from life.

A Young Man, *c*1600, Nicholas Hilliard. This unknown man wears a shirt with turned down collar and centre front opening.

Self portrait, *c*1498, Albrecht Dürer. The artist wears an Italian-style linen shirt with gold braid edging to a wide neckline. It is gathered across the chest with fine pleating.

beginning of the sixteenth century, rising to the Adam's apple by 1530. The revealed edge further protected the gown collar from being soiled.

Ornamentation

Gold and silver, and coloured silk embroidery was developed on all visible areas of the shirt. Portraits reveal how men's shirts and sleeves were pulled through 'slashings' in outer garments by the 1530s. The more debonair and daring gentlemen sometimes provided fuller displays of their under-shirts by leaving their doublets open.

In addition to gold thread edgings and drawn thread work at neck and cuffs, frills of increasingly elaborate lacework gradually developed into a separate ruff during the 1560s. This signalled the start of a trend for detachable lace and linen collars and cuffs, the intricate designs of which mimicked the shirt edgings. Lace in particular became a very desirable but expensive dress accessory. What was owned was therefore ostentatiously displayed.

Smocks for Women

Women's smocks were differently shaped to accommodate the hips by the device of gores let in at each side from just above the waist. Italian smocks of around 1520 appear, from portraits, to have been particularly voluminous with wide, round necklines, finely gathered, and drawn close with ribbon ties. Northern European versions were more restrained. The low square neck of the gown was still echoed by the English smock, which displayed a horizontal frill across the chest from 1520 to 1560, but with the advent of the partlet in-fill to the French gown, which was collared by 1530, and other high-necked gowns, the smock collar began to develop.

Luxury Underwear

A luxury for the rich during this period was a distinct night smock or shirt which was probably much longer than the day version. Mary I's gifts for New Year 1556 included twelve smocks and two night smocks, all elaborately embroidered.[3] For the majority though, the day smock was also worn in bed until the nineteenth century. Yet we know that the gentry had a good supply of underlinen. A contemporary verse advised: 'use your servants as you do your smocks, have many, use one and change often'.[4] Wills reveal that several smocks were owned by ordinary folk, and that by 1550 there were 'hallyday' smocks, indicating special quality garments for best, as well as lesser quality ones for everyday. A 'wedding smock' was mentioned in a poem of the 1640s.[5] A change of linen was important for cleanliness, and several changes facilitated intermittent, rather than everyday, washing.

The Second Skeleton

Already by 1490, understructures were becoming evident in the form of hooped skirts and some sort of stiffened bodice, if not yet a separate corset. These structures gave a new solidity to clothing and started the trend for moulding the figure into unnatural shapes and distorting the silhouette. From the twelfth to the fifteenth century the fullness of the female stomach had been given special significance, perhaps from the religious importance given to childbearing, but from the sixteenth century the emphasis was on a small waist, and an increasingly pointed stomacher which flattened the stomach and created a funnel shape. If there was still a reference to fertility, it was now in the emphasis on the hips as a measure of childbearing ability. The farthingale hoops began to distend skirts, displaying the hems of elaborate jewel-studded velvets and patterned silk brocades and damasks.

The Farthingale Hoop

The farthingale began as a narrow cone-shaped understructure to hold out the skirt which was worn at the Spanish Castilian Court from 1468. Wider versions of this original hoop were taken up in France in the 1530s, in England in the 1540s, and occasionally in Italy. The name derived from the tough and pliant willow-twig hoops (verdugo), also known as osiers, which were covered in cloth such as kersey or buckram and sewn horizontally onto a skirt to make a rigid frame, in wider and wider bands from waist to ground. Cane from giant reeds, or bents, which were stiff hollow-stemmed reedy grasses grown on sand dunes, were also used. Rope and twine, or rolls of fabric, could be substituted to produce a cording effect.

No farthingales survive, but we learn from literary references

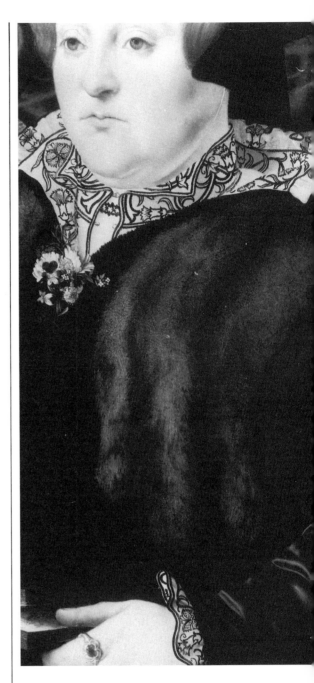

Baroness Dacre (detail), *c*1553-55, Hans Eworth. Cornflowers are embroidered on to the neck of this smock.

17

Mary Tudor, 1544, Master John. Mary Tudor is dressed in a French gown, with a shift just visible, echoing the square neckline. Smock sleeves embroidered in red silk are pulled through separate foresleeves.

that the cone-shaped farthingales gradually become larger in circumference, much to the Church's distress and the amusement of satirists. Robert Crowley described the wasp-waisted Englishwoman in 1550. 'Her mydle braced in, as smal as a wande . . . A bumbe lyke a barrell, wyth whoopes at the skyrte'.[6]

Elizabeth Vernon, Countess of Southampton, *c*1600, British School. The Countess is shown combing her hair in her dressing room, and wears a pair of silk pink bodies with rows of stitching to secure it.

Fleshing out the Form – The Bum Roll

As the cone widened in the 1580s, more support was needed at the waist so bum rolls were introduced over, and often then replaced, the frame. These were cushion pads made of rolls of linen or cotton fustian, filled with cotton wool, and tied around the hips. They were sometimes called 'hip rolls' or hip bolsters. The French called the device a 'hausse-cul'. The term 'bum roll' derived from 'drum roll' and was used by Ben Johnson in *The Poetaster* of 1601. The skirt fullness was concentrated at the back and sides, which gave a half-moon shape variously described as a 'half-farthingale'[7] and 'a semi-circled farthingale'.[8] The rolls remained as alternatives or were worn in addition to the new drum farthingale which developed in the 1590s. The less formal the occasion the less sizeable the farthingale structure needed to be.

The French Farthingale

The two-stage encompassing wheel or drum shape was called a French farthingale. It was made from whalebones, or used other stiff struts radiating at right angles from the waist, with horizontal pleated fabric extending from the bodice, and then falling from the outer perimeter of the wheel. The wheel shape, together with the long busk of the boned bodice leaning down on the frame in front, led to the tip-tilted farthingale of 1600–10, up at the back and down at the front, worn with formal dress in a swansong of extravagance before its demise. In 1617 Queen Anne of Denmark was seen wearing a farthingale 1.2 metres (4 feet) wide in the hips.[9]

When the farthingale hoop disappeared from English fashion around 1625 skirts trailed on the ground. Softer skirts in plain silks were usual around 1650 and their internal linings provided sufficient stiffening. A form of bustle created by the gathering to the back and draping of the side skirts, appeared around 1680 and the weight of the heavier-fabric skirts and layers of petticoats eventually led to the reintroduction of a hoop from 1710. The farthingale had, incidentally, persisted at the Spanish Court through to 1700, under the name *garde-infant* (literally, child preserver), in a flattened form.

Dictating Deportment – Busks and Bodies

The fashionable torso shape fluctuated considerably over the

Queen Mary of Modena, *c*1674, Sir Peter Lely. A round-necked smock showing the frill at the neck is worn in this protrait. Its long cascading sleeves show through panels in the gown sleeves and are looped back with jewels. Painterly undress allows a more casual appearance than reality.

two centuries, redefining the natural form. Around 1500, bodices with stiffened linings compressed the bust, making women look flat-chested. Bents were used for the stiffening, sewn in bunches of around 20, into casings which lined the bodice. There was soon a centre busk, a flat piece of organic material such as horn, whalebone or wood, which would hold the torso rigid, but warm to the body temperature. This busk became increasingly long towards 1600.

Bodies stiffened with whalebones sometimes called French bodies were fashionable by the 1590s. These assisted the creation of a long cone form by 1600. Leather bodies were also known. Surviving examples of iron corset forms were probably for physical correction rather than an everyday form of stay.

From the seventeenth century, the boned lining to the bodice was also known as the 'stays'. Bosoms in the early seventeenth century were thrust upwards and sometimes left virtually uncovered, except for a veil of lawn. Stomachs were compressed. An additional development from about 1630 were tabs to the stays, which emphasized a minuscule waist, and splayed out over the hips, increasing in number and length towards 1700. Stays were rigidly boned across the shoulder blades by 1670, and vigorous back lacing ensured a poker-straight back. Children were dressed as miniature adults and also wore lightly-boned stays for figure improvement and correction.

From the 1560s, women also wore waistcoats, which were an informal fashion worn over the smock and under the main garment. Of linen, silk, or flannel, they were lined, quilted, and embroidered, or trimmed with braid or lace. Cotton wool bombast added warmth.

The term 'petticoat' at first referred to an outer visible layer, a highly decorated skirt. The overskirts of gowns were often slit open in front to reveal the petticoat or 'forepart'. With looser closed-front gowns of the later sixteenth century, petticoats became underskirts, worn for warmth, and made of wool.

Virility and Invulnerability – The Codpiece

Men had little in the way of artificial structure to add to their underlinen except for the extraordinarily decorative codpiece of the mid-sixteenth century, based on a medieval design originally worn as protection in warfare. This was sometimes worked on a foundation of leather. Cotton wool padding to the doublet,

A Young Woman Playing a Harpsicord, 1659, Jan Steen. The young woman wears a rod-for-the-back type of stiffened bodice which pulls her shoulders back. The frill of her smock is visible at the neckline.

rather than any understructure, gave the fashionable peascod belly shape. Trunk hose were also padded out with wool. Silk linings to trunk hose, as seen pulled through vertical slashings and panes in the 1560s and 1570s were probably under-lined with linen to protect the silk. Most men by the later seventeenth century wore washable linen breeches linings, tied at the waist and above or below the knee, which prevented abrasion from wool, or damage to silk breeches.

Getting dressed in this period involved putting the smock or shirt over the head, and often drawing the neckline together in various ways with coloured ribbon ties, buttons, or hooks and eyes at the collar. Women's bodies fastened with laces, the left and right bodies being made separately. A servant or relative might assist with back-lacing. Farthingales were tied around the waist, or laced to bodies through eyelet holes and men's hose were laced to their trunk hose.

Care of Undergarments

Shirts and smocks were cut out mainly at home from materials bought at market. Embroidery for the upper classes could be worked by a travelling broderer, and lace would be bought from a merchant. Tailors, silkwomen and embroiderers were permanently employed by royalty. Farthingales and stays were measured up on the person by tailors. As stays became separate understructures around the 1670s, staymaking became a distinct branch of tailoring, and staymakers — *tailleurs de corps* — became established in premises across the country by the eighteenth century. Linen undergarments could be washed frequently, they were durable and hard wearing albeit they creased easily. They were washed by trampling in cold water, then wrung out, and laid out on grass or a hedge to dry. The sun whitened the linen further. Some bleaching and cleansing agents were known, such as stale urine which contains ammonia, and by the seventeenth century lye, an alkaline solution from wood or plant ashes, mixed with water to produce a mixture known as 'buckwash'. Soap was available in the seventeenth century but was expensive and needed hot water, so was not in common use. Grease and stains were removed by rubbing various absorbent powders, from sheep's trotters to bran and chalk, into the spots, in a turpentine mixture.

A Woman Bathing in a Stream, 1654, Rembrandt van Rijn. Rembrandt's wife Saskia was probably the model for this painting of a woman bathing in her smock. This example is very plain, with a wide V-neck opening.

2

1690–1790

The popular image of eighteenth-century ladies' underwear is of huge side hoops holding a vast oblong skirt out at right angles to the waist, which is funnelled almost to vanishing point by stiff cone-shaped stays. In fact, the hoop shape did fluctuate quite considerably during the period, from its introduction in 1710 to its demise in high fashion around 1780, and the stays took a variety of forms. Fashions of 1740 were certainly stiff and angular, but those of 1770 were characterized by more natural and flowing lines. The function of the hooped understructure was to support the weight of the skirt, while the stays ensured a streamlined bodice. Both outergarments were closely moulded over their frames. Underlinen carried out its traditional functions of warmth, modesty and hygiene.

Eighteenth-century wooden doll. The doll is dressed in undergarments of shift, stays and a hoop (left), and then shown in a brocaded silk sack back gown with original buttoned stomacher and underwear (right). These were accurate miniatures of adult clothes.

The Fashion for Hoops

No structured underskirt as such was generally worn between 1690 and 1710, although a few French women wore gum-stiffened petticoats called *criardes* from about 1700. A hoop was first worn with the mantua, a formal gown that was also worn at court. The new fashion reached the provinces within a year. Informal nightgowns and early sacks, both loose gowns for daytime wear, were at first still worn without a hoop, but it soon became unacceptable to walk out in any gown without a hoop. The early hoop resembled a church dome and was said, in 1717, to have been inspired by St Paul's Cathedral.[1]

The hoop gradually metamorphosed, becoming first rounder and fuller, then oval, widthwise, in the 1720s, already some 3.3 metres (11 feet) in circumference. It further widened at the sides to a huge oblong in the 1730s, developing to a reported 7.3 metres (8 yards) wide, according to a satirist of 1753.[2] Surviving examples tend to be more moderate, closer to 1.8 metres (6 feet) wide. Even so, the silhouette is extraordinary, giving an almost two-dimensional effect of a figure slim to the side yet enormously wide front on. The large expanses of flat surface became an ideal way of showing off successive new silk and embroidery designs, especially at Court.

As hoops got bigger to suit fashionable dress styles, petticoats had to be widened and substantially reshaped to stretch over them. The skirt might be attached directly to the larger hoops to facilitate dressing. One would then simply step into the vast structure and hoist it up to a tie at the waist.

The single hoop structure comprised usually three slightly graduated tiers of horizontal circular or later elliptical hoops, of whalebone, cane, or wood. These hoops were individually covered in linen, or cotton, of varying qualities, and then incorporated into a skirt form. Padding was common, to cushion the weight on the hips. There were side slits for access to pockets which were tied on at the waist and highly decorated.

From the 1740s, the single hoop frame was divided into two, for undress, enabling greater manoeuverability. The French term *paniers*, coined in the nineteenth century, aptly describes the basket-like contraptions. These smaller 'pocket' hoops were covered in cotton, each with two or three elliptical canes to hold them out. They covered the hips and shared a waistband.

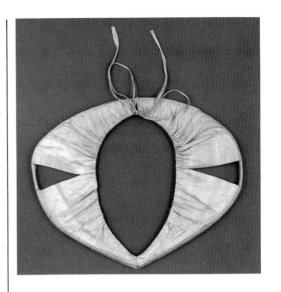

American eighteenth-century hoop. Canvas, stiffened by cane, with slits each side for access to pockets.

American eighteenth-century pocket, *c*1780. Crewel silk embroidery on linen pocket.

Nelly O'Brien, 1762-1764, Joshua Reynolds. The gown is drawn back to reveal the quilted satin petticoat popular at the time.

Petticoats

Quilted petticoats fluctuated between under and outerwear. From 1710 to 1740, they were of plain coloured silks and satins in simple designs, worn under the dress skirt for warmth, and to provide some additional stiffening for the fashionable silhouette. From the 1740s, the front of the formal mantua was often folded back (draped like curtains), the quilted petticoat became fully exposed and the patterns more elaborate. A shorter underpetticoat of stout cotton, plain and narrow, was worn directly covering the legs under the hoops and wider quilted petticoats continued throughout the period for servants and lower orders, perpetuated by a second-hand trade.

In the second half of the century, the fashionable shape in England was often created by these bulky quilted petticoats, displayed or otherwise, instead of the large hoops, or in addition to smaller ones.

Hoops were still worn for a further two decades, but were only very large for formal wear at Court. For other society occasions they might be more moderate and they were left off altogether by 1770. In the 1770s, the looped-up polonaise style of skirt initiated a new fashion for false rumps or more crudely, bottoms or bums. The *cul postiche* made of wool, horsehair, or cork, provided support for the back fullness of skirts. The dress skirt became fully rounded again in the 1780s, falling from a progressively higher waistline, and the rump was cast aside. A small bustle was retained to fill the hollow of the back.

A Graceful Encumbrance? – The Constraints of the Hoop

Hoops took their toll on men's shins in the streets and in dances, and caused numerous breakages. They caused problems in confined spaces such as the theatre, coaches and stairways. They monopolized settees and garden seats. In *The Female Spectator*, 1744, Eliza Haywood wrote that ladies coming into public Assemblies do not walk but straddle, and sometimes run with a frisk and a jump, throw their enormous hoops almost in the faces of those who pass them. Sideways entry through doorways was often the only solution with the formal single rigid hooped structure. However, separate boning for each side of the hooped skirt, together with intricate arrangements of tapes soon enabled vertical raising from the sides, and metal hinges were developed from 1760. But with all fastenings relying on ties, accidents could still happen. Lady Mary Coke recorded in her diary in 1767 how: 'When I came to Leicester House and got out of my Chair, my hoop fell down'! Her friends laughed, and a maid was sent for, to 'tye my hoop'.[3]

Stays and the Wasp Waist

The emphasizing of the hips, and subsequent diminution of the waist, was complemented by very rigid stays which compressed the stomach and pushed the bosom forward throughout the period. They were consistently high at back and low in front. In 1720, a long bodice over rigid, cone-like stays was fashionable. The bosom was supported and emphasized, the shoulders were held back and the posture was slender and erect. Tight-lacing for a wasp waist was fashionable around 1775, with the polonaise gown.

Stays were usually made from several layers of sturdy fabric such as linen, canvas and cotton. Leather was also used, mainly by working class women, but also for children's stays and to correct deformities of the body. They were stiffened with whalebone, or such substitutes as reeds and straw, and reinforced with parallel lines of stitching. Typically, vertical lines on shoulder blades, and rounded diagonal contours across the ribs formed the fashionable cone silhouette. Full-boned examples had densely-packed bones in all directions, but in half-boned examples the boning was concentrated on seams and shape-forming contours. Stays were always laced at the back and always had shoulder straps, generally fastening at front with ties through hand stitched eyelet holes on strap and body, and sometimes extra eyelets on the strap for adjustment. Chamois leather under the arms protected the fabric and boning.

Busks continued to be slotted into a front casing. Surviving busks measure 25.4cm (10 inches) to 38cm (15 inches) long. Of wood, ivory, whalebone or metal, they are usually flat or triangular, rounded or ridged, and thinner at bottom than top. Ribbon ties at either end generally enabled them to be removed at leisure for flirtation, or comfort in undress. Stays could sometimes be agony to put on and wear. Surviving stays of this period with solid busks sewn in and horizontal metal strips across the chest on examples examined, give credibility to this record of agony in the cause of fashion and to Horace Walpole's

At the Dressing Table, 1727, Jean François De Troy. The woman is showing a bracelet miniature to her suitor, whilst being dressed by her maid who is wearing a sack back dress with long stays.

Two stay busks. The top example is made from sycamore and dated 1783. The verse begins 'when this you see, pray think on me' and has an interlaced heart decoration. The left example, from c1775, shows the Figure of Pocahontas and masonic symbols.

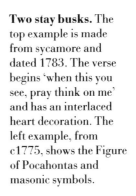

description, in 1777, of a lady 'overturned and terribly bruised by her vulcanian stays. They now wear a steel busk down their middle, and a rail of the same metal across their breasts'.[4]

Stays provided support and warmth, so women did not like to leave their stays off. Some even wore them in bed and in childbirth. These were lightly boned *corps de nuit* or *corsets de nuit*. There were also quilted waistcoats, like sleeveless jackets, which acted as a warm interlining between shift and gown. They were made of silk or linen, quilted and sometimes corded and fastened in front with ribbon ties or lacing.

Shielding the Shape

The shift, still made of linen, was plain throughout the period and the side gores were wider than ever in the mid-century. Decoration where it occurred, was white on white. Towards 1780, the neckline plunged down into a square with rounded corners and sleeves were straight-cut, elbow length, gathered into an arm band. Hand ruffles on smocks remained until the 1730s. The smock sleeve often had worked eyelet holes so that the ruffles could be fastened on with a ribbon.

The Male Perspective

Men's shirts, of fine plain linen with delicate lawn frills, continued their functions as a protective layer for the skin against abrasion and a layer to be washed daily to remove dirt and odours. Cotton and linen mixtures for shirts were introduced from the early eighteenth century, and underwaistcoats of flannel for warmth. Men's drawers were of linen, flannel or leather and instead or in addition, men continued to wear linings to their breeches which were made separately for laundering.

Making and Wearing

Fine quality linen such as holland for shifts and shirts was generally bought in town, and made up by maids. The linen supplier would also make them up if required, particularly quantities of shifts for trousseaux. Locally-grown flax was spun into coarser quality linen at home by wives and daughters. Ready-made quilted petticoats and hoops could be brought. Lower classes made their own stays, or bought second-hand. Makeshift hoops proliferated. Society ladies preferred to have their hoops and stays made to measure. These were made by men until the materials, including boning, became lighter to handle, from the mid-century. Staymakers were also employed to disguise the irregularities of nature.

There were certainly improved standards of cleanliness later in the century. Hot water, boiled up in a copper, and soap were more generally used now for washing linen. Smoothing stones and flat irons were rigorously employed to smooth out the creases. It was more difficult to clean stays. Francis Place described how working class women wore leather stays and camlet petticoats which were 'worn day by day until they were rotten, and never washed'.[5]

Early forms of warehouses, intermediaries between maker and vendor, were being set up and the industry of ready-made understructures was beginning to take form. The industry also brought forth patents for improvements in design such as a woven cloth which looked like stay stitching, for stay cloth, in 1762, and a steel spring for stays in 1784, to allow for expansion across the chest when breathing.

Interieur de la Boutique d'un Tailleur de Corps, c1775, from Leoty, *Le Corset à Travers les Ages*, 1893. Interior of an eighteenth-century workshop showing corsets being cut out.

3

1790–1840

Female underwear and corsetry in this period took a subdued role, following, sustaining and enhancing the lines of the outerwear. There was little embellishment of the shift and petticoat; their purpose was primarily functional. Stays were generally lighter and less structured until the mid-1820s. Petticoats had bodices to sustain their skirts at an artificially high level for much of the period. Shifts and stays were more often known by their French terms, *chemise* and *corset*, from 1790. New undergarments – drawers and corset covers – were entering the fashionable wardrobe by 1840.

The Bare Minimum

Both outerwear and underwear were minimal during the French Revolution (1789-99) and Napoleonic Wars (1800-15). The period began with the pouter-pigeon look, the waistline already raised with the new short-bodied gown and emphasis placed on the bosom which was covered in a wrapping gown and swathed in kerchiefs. Main garments were increasingly influenced by the Neo-classical movement in art which inspired the Grecian statuesque lines of their silhouettes. Rounded breasts and a well rounded figure were considered the ideal and compared with the classical frame of a Venus de Milo shape. In 1793, *The Times* stated that 'the fashion of dressing . . . is to appear 'prominent' and accordingly 'false bosoms' of wadding, also affectionately known as 'bosom friends', were employed by the less well endowed.[1] The substantial painted and printed linens (chintzes) and densely printed cottons of the late 1780s gave way to thin, translucent materials such as fine embroidered muslins and open weave silk gauze, which required opaque underdresses, called 'slips', for decency. There were inevitable tales of too much flesh being revealed, through sparse and transparent garments, particularly in France, in the decadent 1790s.

Caricature by James Gillray, *c*1820. In the early nineteenth century, men's fashion sometimes imitated women's when corsets were worn to achieve the waspwaisted look.

The underwear of 1800 to 1810 remained at the bare minimum required to preserve modesty and uphold the strongly vertical, columnar lines of the fashionable silhouette, now more Roman than Greek – a tubular shift, light stays sufficient to elevate the bosom, full-length petticoat, slip as necessary understudying the diaphanous gown, and, for the ultra-fashionable, optional tight leggings.

A new kind of corset called the 'divorces' which separated the breasts, was patented in France around 1810.[2] This, like many French corsets of the war period, was short-waisted. A notably longer corset prevailed in England, where intelligence about French fashions was impeded by the wars. Also, perhaps, Englishwomen traditionally preferred the longer-waisted style.

The waistline reached an all-time high in 1815. Fashion magazines marvelled that 'the waists are if possible shorter than ever'.[3] The main characteristics of the period 1815-30 were a progressively lower waistline and the development of a bell-shaped skirt. Heavier dress fabrics reappeared, and underlayers multiplied both to support their weight and to sustain the expanding silhouette. The 1820s saw a more relaxed breast position, but the waist was now pinched in by a heavier, more structured and very tightly-laced corset, leading to a wasp-waist silhouette by 1828.

Expansion of hems amused and amazed. A diameter of some 2.71 metres (3 yards) was already claimed by 1834[4]. Four or five petticoats, starched and stiffened, were now required, and there were even reports of light whalebone inserts being used. By 1839, Townsend's *Parisian Fashions* announced that 'horse-hair under petticoats are now almost universally adopted'.[5] This was the horse-hair, called *crin* in France, from which the crinoline skirt was to take its name.

Sleeves to chemises and slips were narrow and short or sleeveless under tubular dress sleeves by 1800. When shoulder puffs appeared in dresses around 1820 underlinen expanded on the shoulder to add support. Full upper sleeve puffs to petticoat bodices held out the increasingly bulbous upper sleeves of the late 1820s. Some sleeve puffs were separate attachments of linen copiously filled with down or feathers. These either narrowed down further or disappeared altogether as the gigot or 'leg of mutton' sleeves collapsed on the upper arm and tightened on a low sleeve line towards 1840.

Progress of the Toilet - The Stays, caricature by James Gillray, 1810. Back-laced stays. These were long line to maintain the fashionable column-like figure.

Lawn drawers, 1820-35. A back view of a pair of early nineteenth-century drawers. One stepped in with the lacing across the back, pulling the strings around to fasten in front with a button.

Linen chemise, 1825. The neckline of this linen chemise is decorated with a lawn frill and pulled close with ties.

Acknowledging the Legs

In addition to the now well-established 'breeches linings' and 'trousers linings', gentlemen wore drawers of cotton, calico or flannel throughout the period, for extra cleanliness, protection and warmth.

Children had worn a form of drawers from the 1780s, variously called 'trowsers' and pantaloons in reference to the male garment, but these were more to cover ankles and knees than to provide any substantial cover for the bottom. Some were only leglets, quite literally separate leggings. Boys up to the age of seven and girls as old as twelve wore drawers under their dresses, with pintucks for letting down as they grew taller. These were frilled where seen. By the 1820s, children's drawers, now more delicately termed pantalettes, were made of thicker fabrics, and were less visible under longer skirts, in accord with a developing attitude of prudery towards the Victorian era.

There are a few illustrations and references to female drawers, 'flesh coloured pantaloons',[5] around 1800 and Princess Charlotte was recorded as wearing them by 1811[6] but it seems that drawers were still rarely worn by women in the 1810s and 1820s. When they finally appeared in some numbers in the 1830s, they were shaped like men's trousers, long and narrow, formed of two separate legs on a single waistband, overlapping in front. Surviving examples are generally of lawn or cotton, with legs to mid calf, cut on the cross, trimmed with pintucks and narrow lace edgings, the waist adjusted with a draw tape or back lacing.

The First Flimsy Layer – From Shift to Chemise

Chemises of this period were still of linen, long to the knee, with traditional side gussets from the hips, gussets under the arms, and short sleeves. Necklines were variously square and rounded to understudy the dresses, and were delicately edged with frills of lawn and lace. Evening chemises were lower cut in a boat shape for décolleté necklines. Chemise necklines of the 1830s were often square, with falling flaps which were now required to cover the fronts and backs of the stiffer corsets. Strings secured these flaps under the arms. Pairs of godets for each breast deepened and widened to hold the fullness of the breasts as they were thrust forwards in the late 1820s.

Chemisettes, which were false chemise fronts, came into

fashion in this period. They fastened with ties around the waist and buttoned at the nape of the neck. They infilled low cut dress necklines for daytime, displaying Ayrshire embroidery and other whitework, where seen.

Petticoats and Slips

Petticoats were made of cotton such as cambric or muslin, flannel, and occasionally linen. They were generally white, sometimes with self-coloured vertical stripes in the weave. Fastening was at centre back with ties, buttons, and hooks and eyes. Hems which might show below the gown were decorated with a simple embroidered design such as a Greek key pattern, or trailing leaf.

From around 1815, tiers of flounces to the petticoat hem developed to further distend the overskirt. As increasing layers of petticoats were introduced, the top petticoat with, or later without a bodice, was starched or given a deep reinforced hem for stiffness. Up to 16 rows of horizontal piping and cording are found on 1830s' petticoat skirts. Pin tucks were usual throughout, for length adjustment.

Coloured slips of pastel pink and blue washing silks in the 1810s, and of a darker shade in the 1820s were semi-underwear only. They acted as foils to diaphanous lace or net or gauze over dresses of contrasting colour. Several different coloured slips might alternate for one elaborate overdress. The hems of slips might have coloured cords or padded rouleaux to maintain the width of the skirt hem, otherwise they added no shaping and little bulk or warmth. These slips may be regarded as early forms of separate dress linings.

Petticoats retained attached bodices until about 1837. Thereafter the petticoat bodice, if still worn, was a separate garment termed a corset cover. It took over the function of providing a buffer for the dress bodice from the exposed upper edge of the corset.

Bustles

Crescent-shaped bustles of glazed cotton or strong silk taffeta padded with straw or cotton wool, or two or three stiffened cotton jean or calico frills were worn to the small of the back in the 1830s to kick out the petticoats. They were tied with tapes

Pauline Bonaparte, Princess Borghese, 1806, Robert Lefèvre. The Princess wears a diaphanous gown over a thin chemise.

Parisian Ladies in Winter Dress, 1799, Anonymous engraving. A caricature of the latest extremes in fashion, transparent fabrics and low necklines.

Ecclesiastical Scrutiny, 1798, Anonymous engraving. Extremes of dress under investigation in this cartoon of 1798.

around the waist in front. The fullness of the chemise skirt was sometimes pulled through the petticoat slit at centre back to simulate the bustle form.

Corsets and the Hourglass Figure

In 1790 all corsets were short, boned, and tabbed around the waist. From 1800-10, whether long in England or short in France, they lost the tabbing, and much of the boning, becoming soft and unstructured except for the central busk. The more daring even dispensed with this. From 1820 they became more sturdy, usually made of a robust twilled cotton or cotton sateen fabric and lined with calico. The finest corsets of 1820-40 were of silk taffeta, corded silk or cotton, stitched with cream silk and subtly embroidered in intricate patterns.

In the early 1830s, the hourglass figure was effected by fuller double godets for the bosoms, square or triangular gussets for the hips, and tight lacing, which on occasions reportedly brought on fainting fits. By 1840, corsets were substantial contraptions, covering bosom, abdomen and hips, rigidified by a steel busk, which was soon known simply as a 'steel', encased in leather, and sophisticated with narrow cross-boning of whalebone and cording. The basic design of corsets now comprised four pieces of fabric plus gussets and shoulder straps. These straps had been wide apart in the 1820s, and were being pushed off the shoulder by the early 1830s to display wide expanses of neck; in 1834 the first strapless corsets were advertised.

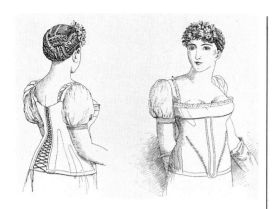

Adjustable maternity corset from *c*1810.

Tight Lacing or Fashion Before Ease, hand-coloured mezzotint, *c*1779, **Bowles and Carver after John Collet.** Stays are worn over a shift, petticoat and pocket in this caricature *previous page.*

Technical Innovations

Steel boning was used in corsets from about 1810. Metal eyelets were introduced in 1828, which enabled tighter lacing without fear of tearing the fabric, although the laces themselves would eventually fray instead.

'Curious Circassian corsettes, with elastic fronts'[7] and 'a long elastic stay'[8] had been offered in 1802 and 1806. Elastic here seems to mean stretchy knitted fabric of silk or cotton.

Various inventions for easier release of corset laces at night were put forward in the 1830s, including a removable rod, a button mechanism, and a spring device. Lacing up in the morning was more difficult, but by 1840 lazy lacing *a la paresseuse* had been introduced, whereby the traditional single lace threaded from top to bottom was replaced by loops of two laces threaded between top and bottom, pulled tight at the waist and tied. In 1829, a front-opening version of the corset with twin steel busks was introduced, and this enabled prearrangement of the back-lacing to individual requirements. Modifications to all these innovations continued for another 30 years.

Special Corsets

Corsets for pregnancy and nursing were unboned, and had button-across bosom gores to allow for feeding. There were also corsets to control embonpoint and other ills of excessive living, such as a 'Bandage Corset and Regenerating and Sleeping Ceinture (which) prevents flatulency, reduces protruberance, supports the stomach and bowels, relieves dropsical symptoms'[9] In 1837, Madam George offered a Calisthenic corset, again 'totally devoid of bone', to enable ladies to undertake difficult Calisthenic exercises, an early forerunner of sports corsets.

Men's Corsets

Hazlitt noted that men had taken to wearing stays around 1820 to give dandies the new fashionable hourglass shape.[10] These were boned and backlaced, like women's. *The Workwoman's Guide* of 1838 lists men's stays for use in the army, for hunting or for heavy exercise. They were to be made of heavy-duty jean, duck, leather or webbing. Such corsets might just be a strip or belt of material, as they did not have to contend with female curves. They were worn between an under-shirt, and an over-shirt or waistcoat.

Getting Dressed

As corsets became easier to lace and unlace, other aspects of getting dressed became more tricky. By 1840, a lady had the daunting prospect of a plethora of tapes, hooks and eyes, and buttons, with a host of undergarments fastening about the waist, including drawers, bustle, pockets, chemisettes, and several petticoats. Many ladies still relied on mothers or maids for assistance in dressing.

Care of Underclothes

A household tradition of holding weekly, monthly and three-monthly washes developed in the late eighteenth century. The more infrequent the wash, the more ostensibly wealthy the family had to be, with so much linen necessary in reserve, and the room to store it. The wash cycle thus became a pointer to social class.

Trousseaux lists in fashionable magazines indicated the ideal number of undergarments required by a lady of society, to support the quarterly wash. *The Lady's Magazine*, November 1837, reported the marriage of the rich Parisian Cecile to the equally rich Viscount Lion de Saint M . . . y. Her trousseau included 6 dozen chemises plus 2 dozen with frills, to wear with riding habits; 4 dozen night ditto; 24 petticoats, sewed to waistbands to form the *pointe* in front; 24 plain ditto. 96 chemises would allow one a day for three months!

Cotton corsets with removable busks could now be washed. Corsets with whalebone or steel sewn in were difficult to clean, hence the importance of such an item as advertised in May 1832: a 'Newly Invented Washing Elastic Stay'.[11]

Making, Mending and Altering

Much underlinen was still made at home, the linen or cotton bought from travelling salesmen. The undergarments were lovingly seamed and trimmed, and later patched and darned as became necessary. A muslin gown would often be turned into a petticoat, cast offs were passed to the poor. Stays could be home-made although *The Workwoman's Guide* advised ordering a custom-made pair from a staymaker first, so that a pattern could then be taken.

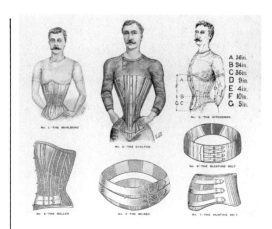

Men's corsets from the mid-nineteenth century.

Fashion plate from *La Belle Assemblée*, February 11 1821. Underwear worn on top in this up-to-date Parisian ball dress.

Fashion plate from *La Belle Assemblée*, February 1815. Ruby merino cloth dress, worn over a cambric petticoat and edged with Valenciennes lace.

Corsets were advertised in pictorial form in fashion magazines from the 1830s, with the discreet image of ladies getting dressed in the privacy of a bedroom or dressing room with a maid, and a clever use of mirrors to show back views.

Fashion plate from *Moda d'Italia Corrière della Dame*, 1823. Glimpses of a lower waistline and expanding hem are illustrated here. The child wears pantalettes with coloured ribbons.

The Stages of the Toilet, French lithograph, *c*1830. Clockwise from top left: the lady wears a chemise and corset, bed jacket over a night chemise, chemise alone, and dressing gown over a chemise *opposite*.

4

1840–1890: Outside In: The Silhouette

This was a period of great innovation and change when dramatic developments in garment style and construction were precipitated, facilitated and in some ways led by technical introductions, such as the innovation of elastic in 1840. Aniline dye colours were available from 1859, producing bright colours such as magenta which had a great impact on stockings and petticoats for informal country wear. From the 1860s, the sewing machine was used in small workshops, outhouses and some domestic homes which led to an increase in the quantity of garments being produced.

Changes in upper fashions affected the styling of a range of well-established undergarments, and led to their being supplemented by a number of new types of underlinen – notably the combination garment. Other undergarments such as the corset cover or camisole and suspender belt were introduced to improve on or modify the function of existing items of underwear. Woollen undergarments which had been employed for winter wear, were often worn all year round. Supports such as crinoline- and bustle-frames promoted more ephemeral fashionable ideals, and did not outlast the century. The shapes of undergarments had to keep pace with all the fashionable changes in waistline and hems, necklines and sleeve shapes. Waistlines began to drop below the normal waist from about 1840. Boning in actual garments had been introduced from the 1830s and in the 1840s was given full reign in dress bodices, to reinforce the shape and pressure exerted by the corset. The waistline began to rise again from 1850 and lighter boning was usual in the bodices of the early 1850s. With the advent of the crinoline frame in 1855, waistlines actually reached a high level not seen since the early 1830s.

After the demise of the crinoline around 1867, the daytime waistline remained high. The bustle sprang from above the small of the back but by the mid-1870s the long cuirass bodice had developed, taking the waistline down to its natural level, drawing attention to female curves and hugging the hips. The bulkiness of the chemise was a disadvantage here, and the new slim combination garment was introduced, partly in response to this tightness of dress. Waistlines remained low into the 1880s and the bustle was much lower slung, jutting out from the bottom of the spine.

Hems habitually swept the floor in the 1840s, early 1850s and late 1870s and yet only a narrow woollen braid was usually provided to catch the mud and dirt, which was more usually soaked and caught up in the petticoats. After the excesses of the elaborate sweeping trains of the late 1870s which must have driven laundresses to despair, *balayeuses* or dust ruffles were introduced in the 1880s.

Fashionable outfits for sporting activities such as croquet, archery, walking and seaside promenading required particularly short skirts which would tend to clear the ankle and often show off the now brightly-coloured and often striped stockings. Skirts might also be looped up around the hem to reveal the under-skirts which spanned their crinoline frames in the 'Pompadour' style, a throw-back to the 1780s' polonaise.

Cartoon from *Punch*, April 19 1879. First Dressmaker 'Do you – a – wear chamois leather underclothing? New customer 'No; certainly not' First Dressmaker 'Oh! Then pray take a seat, and I will send the second dressmaker!' Chamois leather was *de rigueur* for ladies' underwear by 1879: At Madame Aldegond's (Regent Street)

Plunging Necklines

Dress necklines were conventionally high for day and low for evening from the late 1830s through to the 1860s, but always soft and rounded. In the 1870s, they tended to be square, boat- or heart-shaped, and V-shaped or assymetrically draped in the 1880s. Chemise, camisole and nightdress necklines echoed the fashionable shapes. A lady passed through a range of chest-exposing and cover-up necklines in a single day in the 1880s, from a gentle round-necked morning dress to a stiff high-collared afternoon gown, plunge neckline for evening and a high-necked nightdress.

Redefining the Figure – Corsetry

Corsetry of the early- to mid-Victorian period became highly developed. Corsets grew shorter and less tightly drawn in as skirts grew fuller and fuller towards 1855 and might be left off altogether in the late 1850s and early 1860s by the slighter, more erect and more daring ladies, because the contrast between the huge skirts and the ladies' slim waists lessened the need for further accentuation. The earlier tightness of the bodice gave way to folds and pleats running from the shoulders to a central point around the waist allowing chest expansion and more room for the fullness of a chemise, corset and corset cover if required. This was the lull before the second storm of tight lacing.

The Perils of Tight Lacing

Corsets were tighter again and more rigidly formed in the 1870s and 1880s. In the 1840s, the correspondence in ladies' magazines in support of very tight lacing of corsets may have been the product of male fantasies. However, horrific accounts of fainting and giddiness which countered the advocates are very credible. Curvature of the spine, the crushing, displacement, and disease of internal organs, half-developed muscles, difficulties in childbirth such as premature labour, and fatal miscarriages and stillbirths were also blamed upon tight lacing. Amusingly in this connection, reports of hidden (and presumably ultimately successful) pregnancies flourished in the period around 1850-67 when less restrictive lacing and vast skirts allowed a secret to be well-concealed until the last moment.

The clergy and medical profession disapproved strongly of

tight lacing. Commentators of the 1840s drew parallels with the barbaric practice of Chinese footbinding and the reformers of the 1880s attacked the fashionable ideal of women (if not the fetishistic desires of men) which promoted tight lacing, whereas its supporters argued of its benefit not only to the physical state but also to the moral character of women. Back-lacing meant severe strain on the wearer by another pulling strenuously, often with the aid of a knee in the small of the back, to make a 55.9cm (22-inch) waist into a 48.3cm (19-inch) one, even if quoted statistics of 40.6cm (16-inch)-waists are not to believed. Girls were put into corsets or stays from a young age and had to wear them at night to ensure the development of a good figure.

Corsets covers appeared around 1840 and were later termed camisoles. The knitted vests of the 1880s were the winter version of the camisole and were worn over corsets.

The Shrinking Shift

The progressive tightness of the dress bodice in the late 1840s combined with plunging V necklines – dipping down 10.1cm (4 inches) below the navel by 1850 – brought about alternatives for the rather bulky chemise in the form of a false chemise or modesty piece called a chemisette, and separate sleeves attached above the elbow, called *engageantes*. The chemisette was particularly suited to the boat neckline of the late 1830s and the deep V-shapes of the late 1840s.

A Profusion of Petticoats

The lengths of underskirts from the 1830s to the 1850s were clearly carefully measured and adjusted if necessary with pin-tucks, so as not to show below the outer skirt. But the crinoline frame changed all of that. The increasing number and considerable weight of the petticoats fastened around the waist required a frame for support. Fashion at this time was perverse to the point of being unkind: just when it was dictating that skirts should be increasingly wide, so the fabrics of dresses in the late 1830s and early 1840s became increasingly heavy, meaning that several more petticoats would be needed to keep even the same width, especially in winter with heavy flannel petticoats worn for warmth. Starch and horsehair stiffening were used to help maintain the required width. *The New Monthly Belle Assemblée* reported in 1856 that some belles wore 16 petticoats for evening dress. However, a solution to reduce the quantity of petticoats required was obviously necessary. Hence the novel inflatable rubber petticoat advertised as an 'air-tube dress extender.'[1]

Taking the Strain – The Crinoline Frame

Invented by R.C. Milliet of Besancon, and patented in July 1856, this was a skeleton petticoat made of spring steels fastened to tape. The buoyancy of the frame meant that women wore drawers.

The crinoline must be one of the great misnomers of Victorian underwear for technically the crinoline as in 'crinoline petticoats' had long been worn and the cage which we associate with the word meant simply a contraption introduced in 1855-56. The process had begun with the stiff starching of petticoats, which were then reinforced with 'crin' – literally horsehair – in the 1840s. The horsehair was threaded through and this idea was further developed with the insertion into petticoats of graduated hoops of cane or whalebone, and finally, thin flexible steels.

The frame was both a revolution for women and a revelation for onlookers. Women had far greater freedom of movement and the frame was comfortable and light. But the frame also created a new buoyancy and swinging movement which was difficult to control in high winds. Coats, as such, were not feasible. Instead, heavy capes and shawls were worn and these assisted in pressing the skirt closely to the frame, saving and protecting the modesty of the wearer.

The problems with crinoline control were manifold and included getting one's legs tangled in the hoops by taking too generous a step forward, the inconvenience of getting through narrow doors and up tight stairways – in any sense gracefully – and of sitting in confined spaces. Yet crinolines also saved lives: for example the story of a woman whose attempt in 1862 to commit suicide from the Clifton suspension bridge in Bristol was thwarted when she parachuted to safety in her crinoline.

By the 1860s, it became acceptable to show off heavily embroidered petticoat hems, coloured underskirts and brightly coloured – often scarlet – stockings. *The Englishwomen's Domestic Magazine* of 1866 denounced the amount of embroidery upon clothing as sinful.

45

Booth & Fox petticoat, 1880. Petticoat covered in a red paisley print and filled with down for extra firmness and warmth.

Garments from the 1860s. Linen chemise, crinoline cage with red edging, silk corset and petticoat.

The Introduction of Drawers

In the 1800s, drawers were worn by girls but left off by young ladies. In 1841, *The Handbook of the Toilet* recommended them as a fashion already adopted in France: 'drawers are of incalculable advantage to women preventing many of the disorders and indispositions to which British females are subject. The drawers may be made of flannel, calico or cotton, and should reach as far down the leg as possible without their being seen.' The very severe winters of the 1840s may have precipitated their use.

Bloomers

The bloomer costume, launched in 1851 by Amelia Bloomer, to readers of her reform newspaper *The Lily* may have been modelled on a dress worn by ladies in Swiss sanitoriums after partaking in strenuous healthful activities. However, other trousered outfits such as a mountain climbing costume are also cited suggesting various examples and experiments in bifurcated garments at this time. The fashion lasted only six months. The term 'bloomers' passed into the language to describe the closed drawers which emerged several decades later.

Red flannel knickerbockers, 1880-1890. Flannel knickerbockers were popular at the end of the nineteenth century to prevent chills and colds.

The Reception, *c*1881-1885, James Tissot. This fashionable Parisian lady wears her over-bodice on top of the dress in an early example of underwear being worn as outerwear *opposite*.

Inflatable bustle, 1873-74. Made from gutta percha (rubber) in red paisley cotton.

Revival of the Bustle or 'Dress-Improver'

The period of the 1870s and 1880s also saw the introduction of the bustle. Crinolines had become smaller in 1863-7 and were already being abandoned by some. By 1867, they were almost entirely abandoned by the upper classes, not least because every maid, factory girl and peasant in the field seemed to be wearing one. Skirts which were designed to be worn over a crinoline support trailed along the ground and were gradually looped up to form the bustle.

Silhouettes from 1869-73 were often contrived by a series of ties ingeniously placed within the skirt itself which could be gathered up in various sequences. Crinolette frames (half crinolines, concentrated at the back) might be worn with additional pads to give support to these soft bustles. By 1875, the line had become more severe, tighter into the waist, smooth over the hips with the bustle slipping down into knee-level flounces and eventually into a fish-tail train.

The 1880s revival of the bustle after a period of posterior indistinction took a new form, a number of inches lower down. Narrower and angular, it concentrated on the centre back with a horizontal platform which gradually expanded into a 'place-your-tea-cup-on the back' shelf and 'cliff-face' silhouette. It had a complex interior with graduated steels, held together with tapes, lacing and/or elastic and was described by the new seductive terminology of advertising as the 'dress improver'.

Carte de Visite *c*1870. Creasing can be seen at the waist where the dress is stretched tight over the corset of this unknown woman.

The Curtis family of Alton, Hampshire, playing croquet, 1865. Dr Curtis, was a local doctor; his grandfather was Jane Austen's doctor. Glimpses of petticoat can be seen beneath crinoline frames.

This angular silhouette was reinforced by the 'rod-for-the-back' corset which prohibited slouching. The vertical line to the back is the most striking characteristic of the 1880s silhouette. *Sylvia's Home Journal* in 1882 noted a new angularity caused by the fashion dictated that women should 'no longer be swanlike, but square-shouldered . . . suddenly making the English conform to the American outline.' However, there were certain groups of people who refused to wear the crinoline.

Aesthetic Dress
The Pre-Raphaelite Brotherhood, formed in 1848, adopted uncorseted 'aesthetic' dress as seen in Rossetti's paintings of Elizabeth Siddal and Jane Morris. No corsets, crinolines or bustles were worn as a gesture of liberation from the dictates of fashion and a return to more natural modes of dress. *Sylvia's Home Journal* in 1882 mentions an 'Anti-crinoline society' for those who deliberately ignored fashionable silhouettes and also in Great Britain there was an 'Anti-tight-lacing Society'.

The Rational View
The Rational Dress Society, formed in 1881, promoted bifurcated undergarments such as combinations at the International Health Exhibition of 1884, held in London. In April 1888, in the

The Awakening Conscience, 1853, William Holman Hunt. She wears a long cotton petticoat, trimmed with tucks and *broderie anglaise.*

first issue of its magazine *Gazette*, Lady Harberton recommended that the maximum weight for under-clothing should be 3.2 kg (7 lb). It put forward its own rational system of underclothing: 'vest and drawers (or combinations) of wool, silk or the material called "cellular cloth"; a bodice of some firm material made high to the throat, to support the bust and enable such garments as fasten round the waist to be buttoned on to it; the chemise (sometimes called the "Survival"); a divided skirt made in whatever shape or material the individual may prefer; over this the ordinary dress.' The corset was to be left off. The society protested against crinolines or crinolettes as being ugly and deforming.

Health and Sport

The Healthy and Artistic Dress Union was formed in 1890 and in 1893 published *Aglaia*, a journal which included such articles as 'Corset Wearing: the Medical Side of the Attack'. Dr Gustav Jaeger, a Professor of Zoology and Physiology at the University of Stuttgart, believed that wool was the most efficient material to wear next to the skin as its porous nature enabled 'noxious exhalations' to disperse.[2] Wearing wool next to the skin had been advocated by doctors since before 1850 – hence the flannel petticoat. Dr Jaeger advised replacing flannel with an unbleached hand- or machine-knitted wool shirt and drawers or a combination sanitary woollen corset. The introduction of the safety bicycle in 1885 was a leap forward in the move towards women's liberation, allowing freedom of movement and the introduction of more rational clothing. For cycling, woollen combinations, a flannel bodice in place of a corset and a pair of knickerbockers or cloth trousers buttoned on to the bodice could be worn.

— 5 —
1840–90: Inside Out: The Undergarments

In 1840, a wealthy lady might have worn a linen chemise, corset, white stockings, garters, a bustle pad in the small of the back,. several waist petticoats, including one with a bodice and stiffened hem and optional flannel layers for warmth; in 1860: a cotton chemise, corset, coloured stockings, garters, a pair of drawers, a corset cover, waist petticoat close to the legs, crinoline frame, another petticoat and optional flannel layers; in 1885: chemise, corset, stockings garters, drawers or combination garment, petticoat, bustle frame and optional woollen knitwear. A man, on the other hand, had a much easier time: in 1850, he would have sported a shirt and loose cotton drawers. By 1890, he wore either long woven or knitted drawers and vest, or a combination garment with a shirt over. Corsets or belts were an option for sport and figure control.

Materials, Cut and Decoration

Garments were made of linen and increasingly cotton, although initially cotton was considered to be inferior to linen. Cotton cambric, lawn and muslin were the lightest and thinnest cottons and their use became more usual towards 1890. Woollen flannel, which was recommended to prevent influenza, chills and rheumatism was used for winter warmth and soft silks, especially thin silks like China silk, prettily trimmed with lace, hand-embroidered and threaded with ribbon, became popular with society ladies. Leather and chamois leather were among the fabrics used for corsetry, trimmed with lace and machine embroidery.

Elastic was used from the late 1840s for the waistbands of men's drawers, braces, women's garters, and then suspenders

Fashion Plate, *c*1860 from *Les Modes Parisiennes*. Two jupon corsets comprising a belt with pulley systems for raising the petticoat.

and across the insides of bustles to hold them rigid. Horsehair was widely used for stiffening. The sewing machine encouraged more fanciful, all-over patterns with the insertion of several yards of narrow lengths of machine embroidery and lace.

Boning and Fastenings

Boning was provided by whalebone which gradually became increasngly rare and expensive as demand grew. Alternatives included cord or string, and steel once it had proved sufficiently flexible. Other substitutes included rattan, horn and turkey quills. Nothing, however, replaced whalebone for snobbery value with its superior strength and flexibility: the label *veritable baleine* (real whalebone) was held up as a mark of overall quality.

Undergarments became more tailored. Gores were introduced in petticoats from the 1860s and a more complex arrangement of piecing for corsets was introduced. Fastenings usually comprised buttons, drawstrings, tapes or ribbons and occasionally hooks and eyes. Back fastenings to petticoats, corset covers and corsets were common from 1840 to 1856 until front fastening eased the problem of dressing oneself.

Colours, Patterns and Trims

Formal underwear was generally white with more colourful garments being worn informally. Scarlet red was especially

Detail of petticoat, *c*1858-62. Detail of the striking braid trim to a twilled cotton and wool petticoat.

popular for ladies' flannel petticoats, vests and drawers. Flannel for men was usually a distinctive yellowy cream colour. Particular colours identify successive decades: turquoise was popular in the 1870s, grey, green, navy and maroon red in the 1880s. Dense, multi-coloured paisley patterns and printed fabrics appeared on quilted petticoats and bustles in the 1870s.

Decoration began on hems and cuffs and gradually encroached upon larger areas of petticoats, bodices and drawers by 1890. Hand-worked broderie anglaise was popular in the 1850s, with free-style coloured embroidery and braid trimming in strong contrasting colours in the 1860s, followed by machine embroidery and torchon lace from the 1870s. Insertion of embroidery and lace into the main body of the undergarment became popular in the 1870s.

The Garments

Chemise

Many surviving examples are entirely handsewn, with exquisitely over-worked seams. Many are probably homemade although readymades were on the market by 1840 and possibly even earlier. The basic double rectangle with underarm gussets and side gussets was developed and modified becoming less voluminous and less plain with the chemise generally becoming shorter with more shaping to the bust. A less bulky alternative was the Princess petticoat and combinations which were ideal for low-cut figure-hugging cuirass bodices in the evening.

Petticoats

Two types predominated. One was full-length with a back-fastening bodice and deep waistband, shaped to the bosom and with a full skirt. The other was a waist petticoat pleated to a wide waistband.

Petticoats of the 1840s were layered one on another – usually four to six to create the bell-shaped foundation for the dress skirt. While any or all layers might be starched, the outermost layer was more elaborate with extra stiffening, horizontal piping and cording, using cotton wool or string sewn in. Petticoat flounces became deeper and more pronounced to give an extra boost to skirt fullness.

Plate from the *Young Ladies' Journal*, 1879. Dress Petticoat with back tie, back gathering and flounced train.

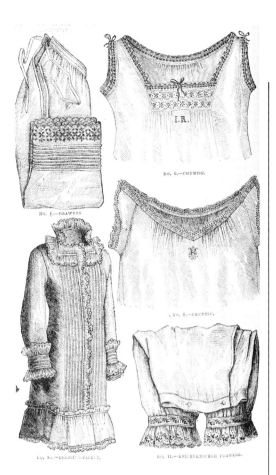

NO. 5.—DRAWERS.

NO. 6.—CHEMISE.

NO. 8.—CHEMISE.

NO. 10.—DRESSING-JACKET.

NO. 11.—KNICKERBOCKER DRAWERS.

Magazine illustration from the *Young Ladies Journal*, 1879. A selection of undergarments which includes chemises, drawers, nightdress and dressing jackets, trimmed with torchon, tucks, lace, insertion and embroidery. Open drawers and closed knickerbocker drawers are both folded for modesty.

Print from the 1860s. Falling out of a bus was just one of the perils encountered when wearing a crinoline *opposite*.

The lady's store of petticoats had to be mixed for various occasions. In 1873, the pamphlet, *A Lady on How to Dress on £15 per year* advised 'three or four good calico, and a muslin one for evening wear, a couple of coloured ones and a strong linsey [wool]'. Trained petticoats provided the foundation for the fishtail trains of fashion, and were elaborately starched, flounced and trimmed. Sometimes the train was separate and buttoned on for formal evening wear, allowing greater versatility and ease of cleaning.

Petticoats were also designed for warmth. Large numbers of post-1865 duck- or eider-down filled cotton petticoats with vibrant multi-coloured paisley prints survive. The prize-winning Booth and Fox examples from the 1880s, models of their kind, were machine stitched with the words 'Russian Arctic' reassuring the wearer of adequate protection.

Plate from *Frank Leslie's Monthly Magazine*, May 1863. Steel and horsehair petticoat, with horsehair flounce to the hem which measures 144 inches (*below*).

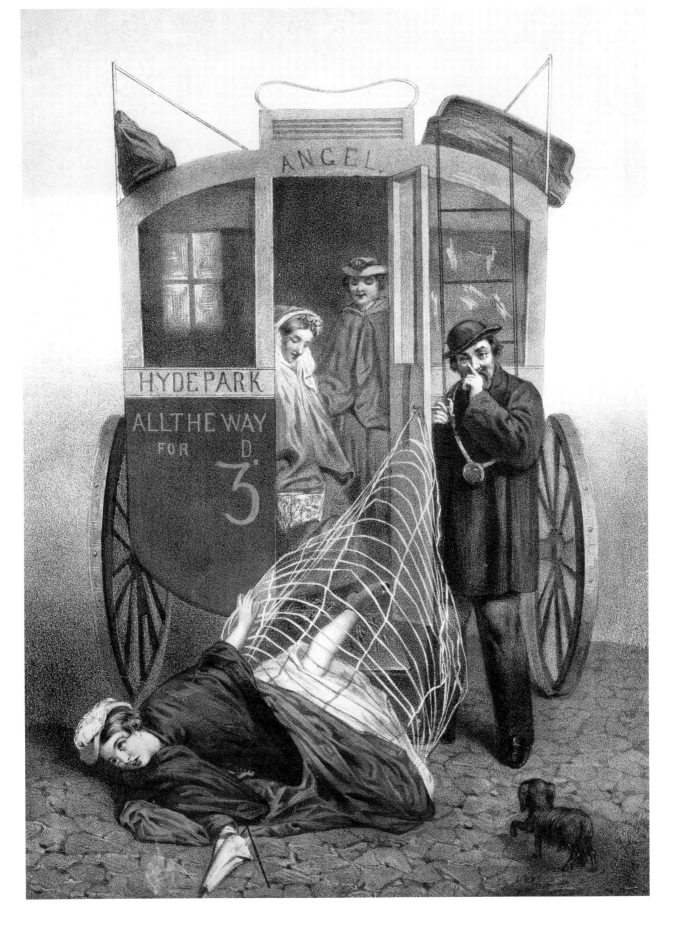

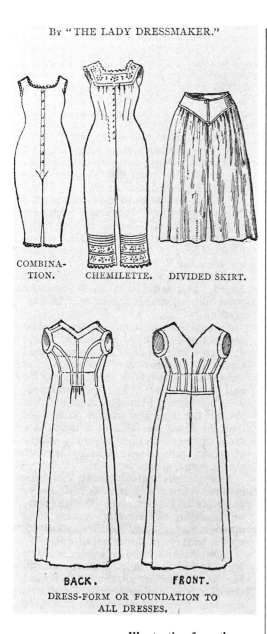

By "THE LADY DRESSMAKER."

COMBINA-
TION. CHEMILETTE. DIVIDED SKIRT.

BACK. FRONT.
DRESS-FORM OR FOUNDATION TO
ALL DRESSES.

**Illustration from the
Girl's Own Paper,
*c*1890.** Reform dress
included combinations, a
chemilette, divided skirt
and a dress form or
foundation in the 1890s.

Bust Improvers

False bosoms of cotton wool were sewn into dress bodices rather
like padded bras today. *Punch*, in February 1877, quoted a
leading ladies' journal which suggested: 'Buy a pair of Mainte-
non corsets, fitting your waist measure . . . put the corset on and
fill the vacant space with fine jeweller's wool, then tack on a
piece of soft silk or cambric over the bust thus formed.'

Drawers and Combinations

In 1840, drawers were still gussetless – just two tubular legs set
onto a waistband – with ties at the front, or gathered over a
waist drawstring which overlapped at the front waist.

Closed drawers, which had the inside seams sewn together to
close the crotch were known at first as knickerbockers and as
knickerbocker drawers by 1879. The legs of open and closed
drawers were cut full and wide but the former were straighter
with the latter being gathered with a frill to the knee. They were
made of cambric for everyday wear, muslin for evening and
flannel for warmth.

The combination combined a chemise or corset cover with
drawers. Originally made of cotton they fastened with buttons to
the centre front and back flap, later being made of knitted wool
too. They reduced the previous bulkiness of underwear considerably. Men wore combinations from the 1880s, in a style
very similar to the female garment. Vests for both sexes were
introduced in the 1840s.

Frames and Bustles

A skeleton of horizontal and vertical steels covered with fabric,
the day version of the frame was short, narrow and cone-shaped
and the evening one larger with a full support to the back train.
In 1860, the circumference of the hoops reached a cumbersome
size (as much as 6 metres (18 feet)). Coverings for the metal of
the crinoline frame were also introduced: 'Those with gingham
or mohair coverings are better than those covered with calico,
which soon gets cut at the bottom by the steel. It is a good plan to
save the last of flannel and tack it on the bottom steel, laying on
that again a piece of strong tape; by this means you will prevent
the sharp edge of the steel from cutting through the material and
also from injuring your boots.'[1] Crinolines were also made of
buckram and split sugar cane. These developed into the

crinolette (half hoops at the back only) and eventually the bustle.

A good bustle was lightweight, firm in shape and flexible. In the 1870s they were made from cotton, linen and a silk covering with horsehair in the weave of the cotton wire. Fillings could be straw, cotton wool or feathers.

Corsetry Contraptions

Corsets were made from strong twilled cotton or cotton sateen. White at first, then fawn and grey corsets appeared from 1850-60. Stiffened with whalebone, they had breast and hip gussets with a busk to slim the waist and support or emphasize the breasts. From the 1880s, corsets became more glamorous — made of satin and figured silk in black with coloured silks, lace and ribbon trimmings to the top edge.

The 1870s was a period of new inventions and patents: spoon busks were introduced in 1873 to equalize pressure on the stomach. There were steam-moulded corsets and corsets with straps, buttons and buckles at the base for attaching other garments. Boning covered with strips of leather was fashionable in the 1880s to increase durability and flexibility.

Corsets with suspenders (now known as the 'basque') were registered by E. William Rushton, Landport, Hants., in 1883. Garters were replaced by stockings and sock suspenders from 1880 with four attachments for stockings and two buttons to fasten at the waist. Only the poorest classes wore stockings tied below the knee with cord, tapes and bits of string.

Maternity corsets incorporated gestation stays, adjustable hip gores and openings to allow breast feeding.

Men wore abdominal corsets into the 1840s to achieve the 'pouter-pigeon' look but left them off from the 1850s except in the military where they continued to be worn. They were also worn for sports such as horseriding and for back injuries. Women wore abdominal corsets with belts, straps and buckles over the abdomen to disguise plump tummies. Women and children also wore shoulder braces to correct posture.

Label from a corset box *c*1880. The 'Quality Tennis Corset' by S & S Sterling Oriental, reflected the growing concern for health and comfort.

— 6 —

1840–90: Round About: Wearing, Making and the Industry

Dressing and undressing, as in earlier periods, were complicated by the excessive layers and extravagance of design in petticoats, and by the addition of successive frame supports. With separate pockets, drawers, and chemisettes all fastening around the waist, there were many ties and buttons to be fiddled with. As each new garment came into use, from corset cover to princess petticoat, combination and button-back knickerbockers and drawers, the tie methods of fastening had to be practised and mastered. At the same time, such expediences as front-fastening corsets, lazy-lacing and elastic made life a little easier. More garments fastened in front, leading to less reliance on maids, except among the upper classes. Back-fastening of dresses became a status symbol, a sign of wealth and good breeding.

The Monstrous Crinoline

Many reminiscences of the problems of wearing the underwear of the period are recalled in autobiographies. Princess Metternich wrote in the 1860s that: 'to walk with so immense a paraphernalia around one was not very easy . . . to be able to sit so as not to cause the rebellious springs to fly open required a miracle of precision. To ascend a carriage . . . required a great deal of time . . . and much patience.'

Queen Victoria told her people she did not like the crinoline frame which she thought 'indelicate, expensive, dangerous and hideous'[1] and adamantly refused to wear one, preferring the traditional bulky layers of petticoats.

Cartoons, newspaper reports and industry statistics illuminate the problems. Ladies fell from carriages and got stuck in

Inflatable crinoline, 1860. Inflatable crinolines were a short-lived fad. Air was blown in by means of a small foot-pump.

58

A crinoline shop in Paris, 1862. 'Huge unwieldy hen-coops hang out of doors of the cheap "selling off" shops . . . They swing about and block the pavements.' The shop assistants in this shop are wearing crinoline frames as well as selling them.

Magazine advertisement from the *Young Ladies' Journal,* **1888.** These health braided wire bustles illustrate the increased emphasis on health apparent by the 1880s.

doorways. An advertisement for the 'Ondina waved crinoline' incidentally pointed up the usual hazards of the frame to a lady's modesty: 'So perfect are the wave-like bands that a lady may ascend a steep stair, lean against a table, throw herself into an armchair, pass to a stall in the opera, or occupy a fourth seat in a carriage without inconvenience to herself or provoking the rude remarks of the observers.'

There were tales of ladies who got caught up in passing traffic and who were killed by standing too close to the fire because their frames acted as tents for the flames once stray sparks had caught them alight. A tale of frames saving lives was reported in America, in the *Hampshire Gazette* of 6 May 1862, of ladies kept afloat in the sea until rescued after a rowing boat accident.

The crinoline frame caused chaos: maids sent chairs flying and knocked precious china from occasional tables and were in danger of showing their all when cleaning doorsteps. Thefts were

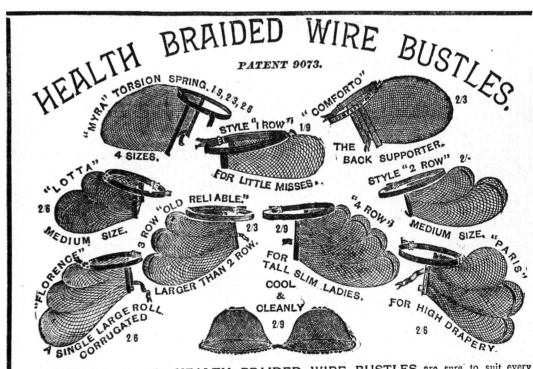

HEALTH BRAIDED WIRE BUSTLES.

PATENT 9073.

"MYRA" TORSION SPRING. 1/9, 2/3, 2/6

STYLE "1 ROW" 1/9

"COMFORTO"

2/3

THE BACK SUPPORTER.

4 SIZES.

FOR LITTLE MISSES.

STYLE "2 ROW" 2/-

"LOTTA"

2/6

MEDIUM SIZE.

3 ROW "OLD RELIABLE."

2/3

2/9

"4 ROW"

MEDIUM SIZE. "PARIS"

"FLORENCE"

LARGER THAN 2 ROW.

FOR TALL SLIM LADIES. COOL & CLEANLY 2/9

FOR HIGH DRAPERY.

2/6

A SINGLE LARGE ROLL CORRUGATED 2/6

DEALERS who keep the **HEALTH BRAIDED WIRE BUSTLES** are sure to suit every Customer, because they are made to conform to all prevailing styles and tastes in dress. They are the **LIGHTEST, STRONGEST,** and most **PLIABLE** Bustles made. They yield to the slightest pressure, yet immediately return to their proper shape after the severest usage, and they properly sustain the heaviest drapery, so that the wearers are never mortified by their being crushed, or bent into ridiculous shapes. These Bustles are Remodelled frequently from the best shapes in the fashionable world, and Ladies wearing them can be sure that, while preserving their health, they are wearing the latest and most tasteful shapes. Sold by all Drapers and Ladies' Outfitters. If you cannot find them, we will send Samples, Post Free, on receipt of above Prices.—**THE AMERICAN BRAIDED WIRE CO.,** 64, Church St., Shoreditch, London, E.

perpetrated under the disguise of the crinoline according to a cartoon in an 1860 issue of *Punch*. In 1860, the textiles firm Courtaulds wisely published a bill prohibiting the wearing of crinolines in any of their factories and mills.

Bustle Memories

Bustles too caused considerable comment: Princess Marie Louise described 'a strange and rather terrible thing, namely a sort of exaggerated pin-cushion stuffed with horsehair... It was meant, I suppose, to give what the dressmaker described as a finish and correct set to the back of one's dress.'[2] There were stories of bustles of the 1880s being formed of rolled-up newspapers or old rags which could embarrass the wearer by falling to the ground if not securely fixed. Make-shift bustles were nothing new: back in the 1830s a maid had been reported wearing three kitchen dusters pinned on as a substitute for a bustle of the earlier style. There is also the story of a lady out walking in Chester who was set upon by a donkey because her bustle was stuffed with bran.[3]

Advertisement from the *Young Ladies' Journal*, May 1877. Izod's patent steam moulded corsets were 'moulded by steam... upon properly proportioned models of either earthenware or metal, in which the respiration of the lungs has been especially considered'.

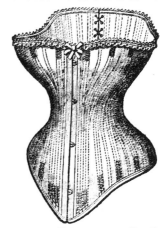

Corsets were chiefly disliked for being too tight, both by wearers, and by advocates of dress reform. Whalebone snapped quite easily under pressure and spare stays had to be kept ready for insertion at any moment.

Washing and Cleaning

The washing of corsets was not advised as they were too thick and heavy to dry easily and the stiffening of whalebone or early rustless steels would have been adversely affected by water immersion. Instead they were cocooned between washable layers of chemise or combinations. Traditionally a pair of stays were made to measure and after a few wearings moulded themselves perfectly to the shape of the wearer. This was difficult to regain if over-cleaned even by dry-cleaning which was generally available by the 1870s.

Stain removal involved spot cleaning with gin, hence the saying 'gin is a mother's tipple', or some other alcoholic mixture. Underarm stains to silk ballgowns worn for dancing were minimized once dress preservers were introduced in the early 1840s, these were tacked inside the dress. Perfumed sachets were available from 1865 up to the 1880s.

Bleaching was undertaken with saltpetre or borax, a chemical compound added to the washing water to give a clean whiteness to underlinen and later a blue block or ultramarine was added to the last rinse for additional whiteness. Starch was used in preparation for ironing. It was made from potato or, after the

Advertisement from *The Season*, November 1884. Twelve figure types were distinguished in this advertisement, in an early move towards hipspring measurements and cup sizing.

3rd Type of Figure.
SWANBILL BELT CORSET,
21s., 31s. 6d., and 42s.
Black, 25s. 6d.

4th Type of Figure.
SWANBILL CORSET,
Black Woven, 14s. 6d.
Black Satin, 21s. and 31s. 6d.

9th Type of figure.
SWANBILL CORSET,
With Regulating Sides, and for Nursing, 21s.
Swanbill Accouchement Belts, 21s.

6th Type of Figure.
SWANBILL CORSET,
For short, stout figures, 14s. 6d.
With Jeanne d'Arc Belt, 21s.

Send Size of Waist with P.O.O. on Burlington House, Piccadilly. Ladies are requested to write for the new Key of 50 varieties of Swanbill and other French Corsets, illustrated by twelve types of figures, sent grat and post free. Cheques crossed London and Westminster Bank, St. James's Square.

ADDLEY BOURNE, LADIES' WAREHOUSE, 37, PICCADILLY, W

Irish potato famine of the 1840s, from rice or wheat or horse-chestnuts. Starch was also used in the process of steam moulding corsets in factories from the late 1870s.

Ready-Made Garments

Ready-made corsets were available from at least the 1830s and bustles from the 1840. Stay stitchers and gorers were employed in a factory in Portsmouth as early as 1846. At this date, the women would have cut and sewn in the gores and stitched up the whole corset by hand. Many still worked from home as outworkers. By the 1860s, staymakers were introducing sewing machines into their factories and by the 1840s, ready-made underlinen could be bought from ladies' outfitters.

Developing technology aided the production of garments. The band knife developed between 1858 and 1860, was able to slice through several thicknesses of material enabling garments to be cut out in batches. The business of corsetry became much more technical after 1862, when Edwin Izod of Portsmouth developed a testing machine to test the behaviour of metals under impact in order to improve corset steels. Rustless and unbreakable steels were being developed and there were many claims to their discovery.

The English corset industry developed into a huge concern, taking orders from the USA and France. From the late 1870s, corsets were attractively packaged in boxes with decorative and often coloured labels. Early advertisements in newspapers and fashion magazines appeared as line drawings and as the occasional hand-coloured-fashion plate. Drawers were rather shyly drawn – folded with just parts of the embroidery or lace showing. From the 1870s, there was large-scale advertising of underclothes and corsets, and, in the late 1880s, advertisements became more and more explicit to match the luxury and erotic appeal of the garments.

Ladies could buy underwear from large department stores like Swan and Edgar in London or by mail-order from companies, such as Sears Roebuck of Chicago and Great Universal Stores in the USA. Early selling of ready-to-wear underwear was promoted by the use of royal names such as 'Dagmar' tagged to specific designs for chemise petticoats and even a corset – the Princess Beatrice Corset, but not for drawers. This would have been just too indelicate. Corsets were also given exciting and fanciful names to attract their clientèle. Some examples include Rosenthal's Postulata, 1884; Dr Warner's Coraline, 1888; and Brown's Dermathistic, 1887.

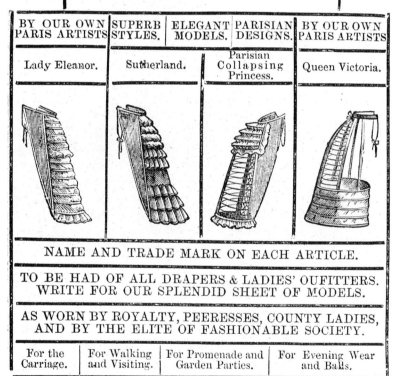

Magazine advertisement from *The World of Fashion*, 1885. Skinner's tournures, crinolettes and crinolines. As worn by the elite of fashionable society.

SCENE ON THE SANDS.
Master Tommy won't go in the sea.

Advertisement for Harness's Magnetic Corset, c1888-92. Extravagant claims were made as to the benefits of corsets such as these.

Postcards of crinolines, c1880s The impracticality of crinolines was a common subject for ridicule.

Miss Barepole in the late Gale.
With topsails carried away.

— 7 —

1890–1940: Outside In: The Silhouette

Photographic postcard, *c*1904. Miss Gabrielle Ray displays her petticoats.

The Era of Lingerie

The period of the Belle Epoque from 1890 to 1913 saw extravagant and conspicuous consumption in women's dress generally, and in underwear especially. This was now much lighter in appearance, weight and feel, but altogether more luxurious and glamorous in conception and more exquisite and delicate in execution. Mid-Victorian underwear seems lack-lustre, utilitarian and heavy by contrast. New luxury under-garments were now made in sets including nightwear and were given the group name 'lingerie' from *'linge'* the French word for linen.

Serviceable cotton longcloth and flannel gave way to cambrics, merino and silks. Metres of lace and embroidery insertion characterized the Edwardian array of lingerie. While the 1920s saw a paring away of excess, hand-made lingerie with lavish embroideries and lace trimmings was still the order of the day for the rich, and the best lingerie was undoubtedly to be had in Paris. It was only in the economic slump of the 1930s that mass-produced machine-made lingerie in rayon became more socially acceptable.

The Controlling Corset

Under the froth of lingerie, corsetry was all-important in procuring the fashionable shape, erasing unsightly bulges as required. The waist was fashionably minuscule throughout the 1890s in order to place emphasis on the bust and the hips. This wasp-waist fashion relied on the tight-lacing of the corset for full effect. The famous S-bend look of Camille Clifford, the English 'Gibson Girl',[1] promoted from around 1900, was copied throughout the country. Photographs of fashion idols were doctored to make waists look even smaller, and both bosom and bottom even larger, to erotic effect.

The waist rose again around 1907 and sat just above the natural line throughout the war. A rigid sub-structure was still very necessary, but now that the S-bend had been shown to distort the spine, straight, long-line corsets, some 50 cm (20 inches) deep, were in vogue. The main emphasis had shifted to the hips, which were enlarged and controlled by lacing at back and sometimes also at the front to create the desired perfectly smooth line. With the shift in emphasis from the waist, measurements there relaxed up to 70 cm (24 inches) by the late Edwardian period. Paradoxically, the French designer Paul Poiret, who pioneered the long 'empire' line from 1908, which led most women to seek out a well-boned corset in order to achieve this, developed a boneless corset in 1911 and actually forbade his own wife to wear any corset at all.

By 1910, Spirella's corsets had large bust gussets and a deep back curve which gave the unnatural 'Kangaroo' look. By 1912 the bust was made slightly larger than the hip to give the hipless look of the hobble skirt period.

The 'brassière' was initially introduced as a cover for the bare bosom, rather than as a support for the breasts. It could be worn beneath, or as an alternative to the chemise. As the corset dropped further and further down towards the waist, the need for another garment became increasingly acute and various alternatives were offered. The fashionable corset teetered on the nipple line from 1902, falling below the bust by around 1906. Fron 1908, long corsets covering the hips settled their upper edge on the rib-cage just mildly nudging the bust upwards. By 1913, corsets were only 5 cm (2 inches) above the waist. So the original corset covers, now termed camisoles, took on a new and necessary role of bust cover, but they tended to be loose-fitting, unsupportive, and semi-transparent with voided areas of patterning. A closer-fitting, more supportive and more opaque covering was required for developed chests.

By 1900, the 'bust confiner' or flattener had appeared and this became more important in the 1920s.

In 1904, the word *soutien-gorge* entered the French dictionary. The seed of the idea for separating bust- and hip-controlling corsetry had come in 1889 from the legendary contribution of the Parisian boutique owner Mme Herminie Cadolle, who

Theda Bara in *Cleopatra*, 1917. The film caused an uproar as a result of costumes, so revealing, that it was uncertain whether Bara was wearing any underwear at all.

decided to cut the midriff out of the full-length corset to allow more movement from the waist. Her invention was first termed *corselet-ceinture*, then *corselet-gorge*. The term 'brassière' first appeared in American *Vogue* in 1907, and in English magazines by 1912. In 1913, Caresse Crosby in New York used two triangles to form a brassière for an evening gown, and the idea was bought by Warner for $1,500.

The bra contributed to the re-emergence of the breasts. In 1930, Pregermain produced a strapless bra and after Gertrude Lawrence appeared on stage in *Private Lives* (1930) in a backless dress this vogue was followed by all classes. The cinema also brought fashion to the High Street: Mae West, playing Diamond Lil in 1928, wore a Spirella corselette with bra cups

Advertisement for Reform underwear, 1892. Reform underwear from the 1890s was strictly practical, and without unnecessary embellishment.

Advertisement for the 'Jurna' corset, 1918. Corsets such as these were worn to maintain the new straight-hipped look.

Advertisement for Warner Brothers Coraline corsets, *c*1890s Corsets for health, nursing, protection of the hips and abdomen were all part of the new concern for healthy undergarments *opposite*.

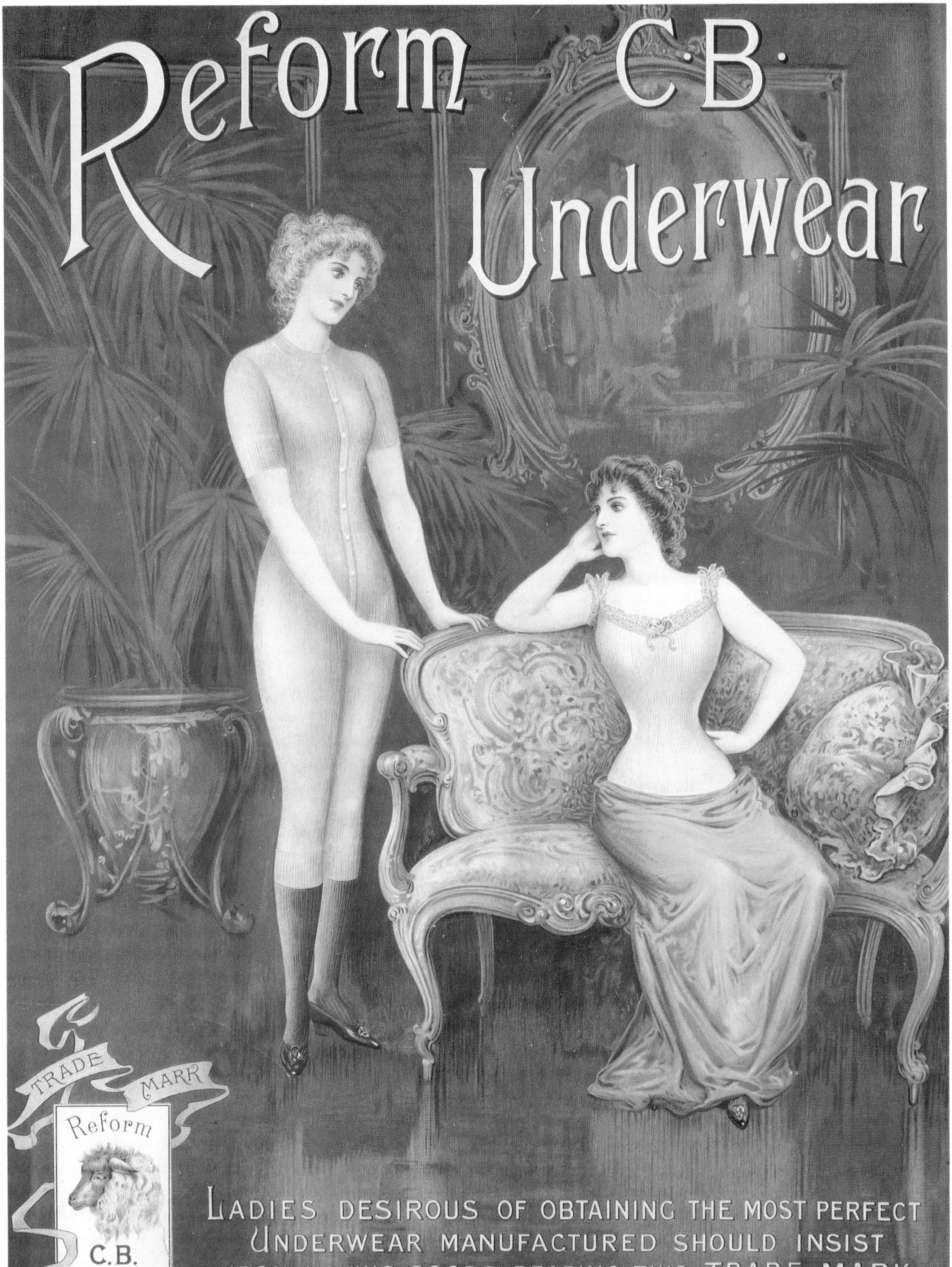
Reform C.B.
Underwear
TRADE MARK
Reform
C.B.
GUARANTEED QUALITY.
LADIES DESIROUS OF OBTAINING THE MOST PERFECT
UNDERWEAR MANUFACTURED SHOULD INSIST
UPON HAVING GOODS BEARING THIS TRADE MARK.

Line drawing from *Le Corset à Travers les Ages*, 1893. Petticoat with full back and vertically pleated hem.

but no back. Also the brassière top on vests, combinations and scanties was sometimes made so close fitting that no other brassière was worn - and yet there was only a brief interlude before another kind of boning became *de rigueur*, the under-wired bra cup which seems to have emerged around 1938-9.

From 1890, hemlines were already shorter – up to the ankle! Skirts were wider, indeed bell-shaped, with additional fullness at the back, allowing women to stride purposefully along. Yet the pre-World War I suffragettes were, ironically, fashion victims indeed in that their rise coincided with the tyranny of the hobble skirt. This fashion once again made walking more difficult and, worn together with the long corsets fashion demanded, showed dress styles sadly lagging behind the suffragettes' ideals of female emancipation.

One important trend was noticeable by 1914: the straighter, slimmer skirts were just perceptibly shorter, rising as much as 4 or 5 cm (1-2 inches) above the ankle. In 1915, the tube shape disappeared and a fuller skirt developed out of the wide overskirt previously worn with the slim skirt. This change was echoed in fuller, shorter petticoats and led to revisions in other undergarment shapes and lengths as well.

1914-27 – Liberation of the Limbs

It was during the First World War (1914-18) that women started wearing trousers to facilitate their active work in munitions factories and on the land. Some Land Army girls abandoned their restrictive corsets, almost literally, in the field. The adoption of trousers by women was made easier by the existence of bifurcated undergarments, which had entered the world of fashion from the late 1880s and which the French called *culottes*. Calf-length knickerbockers adopted for the new craze for cycling had precipitated, or at least echoed, changes in women's drawers. Combinations were already in use, and shorter and wider divided petticoats and camiknickers emerged after 1910. Drawers became closed and shorter, to just above the calf, in keeping with the shorter knickerbocker lengths and continued to rise with the rising skirt lengths. The late introduction of closed drawers almost certainly had something to do with conditions of sanitation: it was not until 1884 that the first public lavatory was opened at Oxford Circus in London. Closed drawers were not thought decent by all; Augustus John would not allow his female relatives to wear closed drawers well into the 1900s.

695 H. Nainsook Camisole, trimmed imitation Torchon lace, 3 frills edged lace across front, puff sleeves, basque, fasten back **18/11** doz.

6021.—Nainsook Camisole (with basque), trimmed Val. lace, wide ribbon insertion, and ribbon, lace shoulder straps. **28/11** doz.

6002.—Camisole to waist only, trimmed Val. lace and insertion, embroidery motifs threaded ribbon   ...   .   **25/9** doz.

Advertisement from Dawson catalogue, 1907-10. The 'mono bosom flounced bust enhancement feature', in various different versions for day and evening, according to gown style.

The Oktis Corset Shields, registered date 19 August 1900. Corset shields consisted of light flat steels in cloth casings which were stitched inside the front of the corset. It was claimed that they 'doubled the life of a corset'.

Seated Woman in a Chemise, 1923, Pablo Picasso. The simple chemise never went completely out of fashion *opposite*.

Coloured postcard, *c*1908 German. Young girl in under-bodice and buttoned-on knickers contemplating a swim in the lake.

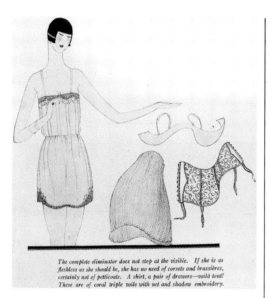

The complete eliminator does not stop at the visible. If she is as fleshless as she should be, she has no need of corsets and brassières, certainly not of petticoats. A shirt, a pair of drawers—voilà tout! These are of coral triple voile with net and shadow embroidery.

Magazine illustration from *Harper's Bazaar*, December 1924. The Complete Eliminator was breaking new ground in the 1920s.

The First World War

The war had an impact on all aspects of life, even underwear. Patriotic feeling during the war was expressed in such quirks as red, white and blue corsets representing the flags of various nations. Diana Cooper ordered for herself 'chemises embroidered in hand-grenades'. Another feature was the increase in knitting and crochet, particularly of underclothes, partly in response to an appeal for warm body belts for the men at the front and, as clothes rationing took effect, in order to keep those at home well clothed.

The succeeding inter-war period saw the 1920s' jaunty, boyish, careless look, then a very overtly sexy period, building up to a crescendo of delight in the lingerie of the 1930s, when surprisingly little corsetry was worn by the young ultra-fashion-conscious.

Hems generally rose from the calf to the knee from 1918 to 1926. Bodices and hems were cut straight across, in the most minimalist phase of fashion ever known, which was particularly severe in Britain. The corsets that existed were often boned only at the sides, with elastic gussets for a smooth hipline and flat tummy. Brassières were in the form of bandeaux which flattened the bosom. Magazines advised women to buy corsets two sizes too small to achieve the desired slim look. The 1920s' slip was a shift-like garment which provided a sheath for the main dress, with minimal shaping and minimal embellishment to keep the slim line.

1927-39 – Curves and Contours

The changing silhouette influenced the shapes and styles of the new garments, for example, the change from a high- to a low-level hip line around 1923 to 1926. From 1927, handkerchief dress hems with ragged edges were seen, echoed in lesser degree by the underslips which began to show undulations of cut. By 1928, there was a full return to curves with emphasis on the hips and hems went back to calf length where they remained until the late 1930s for day, falling back to ankle length for evening.

All-in-one lingerie continued in popularity and although the camisole went out of fashion in the 1920s, its name survived in a

76

range of these combined garments, hence the camiknicker, cami-bocker and cami-petticoat. Camiknickers were recommended for wear with suits to achieve a flowing line and became the most popular undergarment of the 1930s.

By the 1930s, there was a new generation who had never known the strictures of heavily boned corsets, even if they did adopt some form of unboned or lightly boned corselette, girdle or belt or 'step-in' or 'roll-on'. In 1931, a lastex two-way stretch corset called *Le Gant*, which solved the annoying problem of the roll-on riding up, was launched by Warner Bros. Plenty of boned corsets were of course still produced for more matronly figures and for those who would have felt naked without them!

Le Bain au Soir d'Eté, 1892-93, Felix Vallotton. There are echoes of Rembrandt in this painting of women bathing in sleeveless chemises, white drawers, black corsets, black stockings and white petticoats.

Brassière and knickers, 1931-33. Silk figured bra and knickers with the very popular art deco motifs of the era.

Nightdress, chemise and slip, 1935. These undergarments were the prizewinners in a *Daily Mail* competition. The hand stitching was so fine that the work was initially rejected as it was thought to have been made using a machine.

Camiknickers, *c*1920s Dancers make a striking motif on these camiknickers.

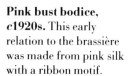

Pink bust bodice, *c*1920s. This early relation to the brassière was made from pink silk with a ribbon motif.

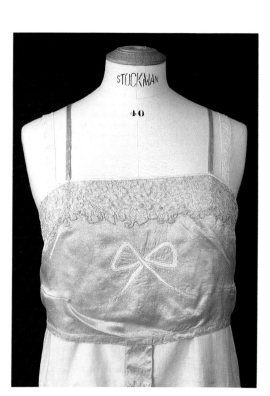

Sitting woman, 1917, Egon Schiele. The artist's model wears a pair of short silk knickers *opposite*.

Health and weight-watching

Health concerns were conspicuous at the beginning of the century. Tight lacing continued to be condemned as were garters because they restricted the circulation and led to varicose veins. However, the main concerns were about dieting and the quest for a healthy body.

The 1920s saw the development of a new, but lasting, concern about weight. This was linked directly to the new level of

A still from the film *The Gay Nineties*, 1930. The intricacies involved in getting dressed in the 1890s are well-illustrated here.

exposure of the limbs with the shorter, sleeveless dress fashions and the new craze for sunbathing. Gradually the connection between slimness and longevity was made and a cult of healthy living developed with diets which cut out starch. A craze for physical fitness and sports activities started, including swimming, skiing, ice-skating, dancing the Charleston, cycling, tennis and tap-dancing. A good figure became more important than a pretty face. Flabbiness was exercised away in classes organized by the Women's League of Health and Beauty, established in 1930 by Molly Bagot-Stack, which had 160,000 members by 1939. Ladies wore white satin blouses and black satin shorts or short pants (and skirts when giving demonstrations).

'Health' corsets which claimed to support the bust and reduce the figure by several inches and assist all abdominal ailments were marketed as were rubber 'reducing' corsets (to encourage weight loss by sweating) by 1924.

Women on the move and in active work faced potential problems with management of the monthly period so in the 1880s Kotex disposable sanitary towels were developed to

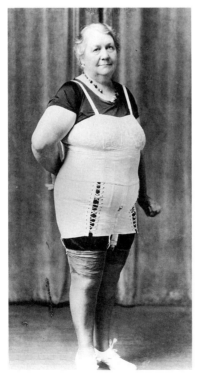

Spirella publicity photographs, April 1937. Spirella corsetry for the mature figure worn over combinations in knitted rayon.

replace the washable napkins used previously. Internal protection (tampons) was available by 1931 – Hollypax, from Hollywood, were available from Woolworths during the Second World War, although the health warning on tampons was not lifted until 1956. However, until the 1920s and 1930s many women still used washable napkins as sanitary towels because this was cheaper.

Sizing – The Triumph of the Individual

Gossard distinguished nine figure types and classified these more generally into slight, average and heavy, with progressively more boning for the back, front and sides in corsets for larger figures, and additional inner belts or surgical elastic to support and control the diaphragm and abdomen.

Berlei's pioneering survey of 1926-28 discovered five different figure types, and the company marketed its corsetry accordingly. This was the first recognition of the supremacy of the natural form over one single rigidly imposed silhouette and led to the introduction of a range of sizings for bras and corsets in the 1930s.

In 1935, Warners introduced A-D sizing, though their claim to have originated this was challenged and led to action in law. In 1937, the company Royal invented the hipspring system, which identified different figure types based on the difference between the measurements of the waist and the hips, from 22 to 33 cm (9-13 inches). Qualified saleswomen/fitters were able to measure their customers and assign the correct shape.

Gossard Catalogue, 1920. A front-lacing corset for the 'ideal average figure' size from Gossard.

— 8 —
1890–1940: Inside Out: Undergarments

This period saw a great change in just what was worn as underwear as well as in its shape and fabric. There was a merging of corsetry and lingerie and a new term 'undies' – part of a general trend towards the abbreviation of underwear names, for example 'bra' (1937).

Typical day lingerie sets comprised, in the 1890s, a fancy chemise and drawers or combinations, a corset with suspenders, black stockings, camisole and one or two petticoats. By 1912, this might have been reduced to a short silk chemise and silk combinations over stockings to the knee and, in the 1920s, consisted of chemise or vest, corset and bandeau or corselette. The 1930s saw vest and knickers or camiknickers worn widely as a set.

Corsets were always worn from 1890-1920. From 1921, corselettes (also known as cami-corsettes) and from 1928, brassière and belt sets might be substituted.

The introduction in the nineteenth century and development by the 1930s of elastane stretch fabrics was revolutionary as far as underwear was concerned. Buying ready-made was becoming more acceptable though many manufacturers' and shop labels were discreetly placed, secreted for instance in the inner fold of the crotch of a pair of drawers, and they were often removed by the customer.

Materials

Rustless steel appeared in corsets in the 1890s and spiral steel bones from 1904-5. By 1922, some corsets sported elastic inserts which made wearing them much more comfortable. At first, the elastic was only available in narrow strips which were joined

together, and at one point sheet rubber was used to make a wrap-around corset, but the real breakthrough came with the production of elastic yarn that could be woven to give two-way stretch. This elastic thread, known as lastex, was developed by the US Rubber Company in the 1930s under the trade-name Spandex.

The staple lingerie fabrics of the period were fine (cotton or linen) cambric and lawn and soft cotton, though pure silk was very popular and artificial (or art) silk began to be used in the 1920s, giving rise to a certain snobbery in those who could afford the 'real thing'. Man-made silk was thought rather nasty, though it at least gave an illusion of luxury.

Silk from the East became more readily available from the 1890s and, in the form of crisp silk tussore petticoats and rustling paper taffetas, successfully created the characteristic Edwardian 'frou-frou'. Crêpe de Chine and Japanese silk were used from 1908 to achieve the new slim line. Being opaque, silk, satin and shantung were popular in the 1920s for wear under diaphanous *mousseline de soie* or chiffon evening frocks. In the late 1920s, silk crêpes for day and sheer transparent triple-weave silks for evening gained favour because of their fluid qualities and because they took appliqué well.

Knitted underwear was made in silk tricot, Milanese silk, silk and wool, and wool. Knitted rayon was available under the trade-name Celanese knit and wooed its public with claims that it was crease resistant and ladder-proof. Knit became more popular after the launch of jersey wool for underwear in the 1890s, its natural elasticity giving added comfort.

Aertex, a trade-name for a British cotton cellular cloth, was created by a company set up in 1888 specifically to manufacture a fabric that would let the body breathe while keeping it cool in summer and warm in winter. It was used for a wide variety of items of underwear including vests and combinations.

Finally, there was still considerable use made of all-over lace for ribbon corsets and bandeaux.

Colours and Decoration

From 1900 to 1914, silks for lingerie were made mostly in white or in pastel colours but after this, new methods of dyeing fabrics in strong colours which would be fast in the wash were developed. Vivid Indian reds and emerald greens appeared (among others), only to give way again to pastel shades from 1923 onwards. Peach was actually the most popular shade of the inter-war years, followed by pink, ivory and eau-de-Nil, but it was the sheer range of colours that was noteworthy: sky, yellow, tabac, heliotrope, coral, ivory, champagne, saxe, vieux rose, cyclamen, apple and black all featured.

Decoration might be integral to the fabric, as for instance with broché (a type of brocade), or added in the form of embroidery, either machine sewn or done by hand: a specialized use of this was made in about 1914 in the shape of beading embroidered on knickers and threaded with ribbon. Embroidery was also used to add popular motifs such as large butterflies to undergarments and to decorate eyelets in the fabric. Drawn thread work was also used as decoration.

Lace was as widely used as ever for insertions and as an edging. Ecru tinted lace made pretty appliqué motifs and appliquéd roses of silk might also be seen on lingerie sets in 1924. Vertical pin tucks remained a standard decoration as did decorative bows on chemises and knickers. Printed decoration of underwear fabrics had appeared in the 1890s but lost popularity over the years 1895-1910, returning in the 1920s and 1930s because it was cheaper than embroidery. It became a rapidly expanding form of underwear decoration in these years. There are extant examples of art deco style printed lingerie items (about 1925-30) and in about 1921, Liberty's advertised an 'underskirt in hand printed Tyrian silk' and in 'hand printed Rani satin'.

The garments

A number of new-named garments as well as changes in silhouette appeared as a result of technical developments, which led to less rigidly formed spiral steels, new forms of elastic, the use of rubber and new fabrics, such as rayon or art silk. These were the brassière, corselette, camiknickers, suspender belts, the teddy and the roll-on.

Underskirts and Petticoats

1902 saw underskirts of rich glacé silk with a flounce edged with a small tucked frill in colours from sky and heliotrope to turquoise and cherry. In another advertisement of that year the

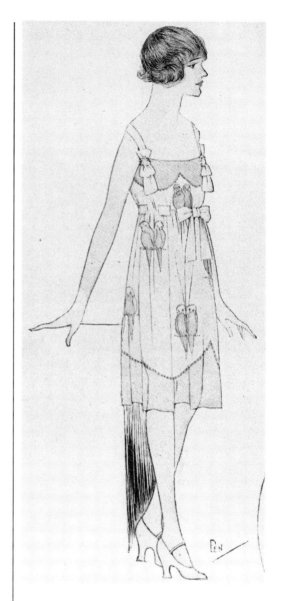

Magazine illustration from the *Tatler* 19 January 1921. Chiffonelle camiknickers, printed with a bird pattern and trimmed with ribbon bows. Long camiknickers looked like a slip, but had a divided skirt and under-crotch gusset.

following were offered: rustling silk at 21s; real tussore washing silk at 16s 9d; linen-finished sateen, batiste or flannelette at 18s 9d. As well as variety of fabrics there was choice of colours – rose pink, cerise, electric, slate, purple, coral, vieux rose and reseda were all on offer.[1]

In 1912, Marshall & Snelgrove advertised underskirts in satin broché, crêpe de Chine, broché poplin, Milanese silk and moiré poplin. During the 1920s, coloured underslips were sometimes worn to complement (and make respectable!) transparent over-dresses of chiffon and georgette.

Petticoats were still very elaborate in the 1890s (though shorter than they had been), with many flounces at the hem, and they came in fabrics as diverse as silk, satin, flannel and alpaca according to need. A winter sale offer of 1892 included cloth, felt, quilted, down and woollen petticoats.[2]

In construction the petticoats of the 1890s were gored and trained at the back, additional material being gathered up at the small of the back to form the foundation for a bustle. As for shape, this was fairly tight in the late 1900s and up to around 1913, flaring out after around 1916 and straight and loose in the 1920s, sometimes with a pleated skirt. Ribbon shoulder straps were common.

While the no-waist look of the 1920s persisted, full-length petticoats were preferred and this continued into the next decade, the skirt flaring from the knee in the early 1930s. These full-length petticoats were called Princess petticoats (after Prin-cess Alexandra), later known as Princess slips and finally slips.

Slips

The slips of the early 1920s were cut so straight that front and back were barely distinguishable. There was no bust darting, just a ribbon tie in front and a slight gathering over the bottom at the back. In fact, slips of this time often gave the appearance of waist petticoats that had been hitched up and tethered at the shoulders by narrow straps, thus creating a stove-pipe shape. In the 1930s, a typical slip might be shaped at the bust and cut on the cross like the bias-cut outerwear it was designed to underlie, with inlet side flares from about 1933-4.

Chemises

The line between the chemise and the slip became blurred around 1920 but where the slip of silk usually had some sort of

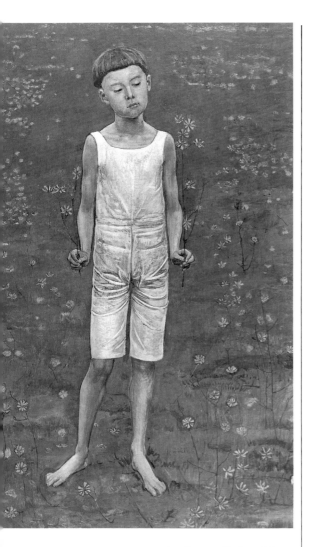

Anebetung Stehend I, 1893, Ferdinand Hodler. Boy wearing vest with button-up drawers, like the American BVD's (union suit) with knee-length rather than full-length legs.

shaping to the torso (for example indication of a waist or hip line), and had a trimmed hem, the chemise tended to be much plainer, though prettier versions were also introduced later in this period.

In 1894, the Cellular Clothing Company was advertising chemises in white cellular cotton trimmed with lace or white lisle, and in 1892, Baroness Staffe referred to 'chemises of printed cambric, or pink, blue and mauve surah' (though she found them 'in somewhat doubtful taste'). The 1890s also saw trimmed frills of embroidery, and fronts with vertical tucks and fancy embroidery. One Harrods model – 'Antique Valenciennes lace' – was sleeveless, held at the shoulder by ribbon and buttons and simply gathered just under the bust line, and in *Home Chat* for 1 August 1914 a 'quite new chemise pattern' with a high waist, no sleeve and a V-neck is described.

Traditionally of cotton or linen, chemises also came in silk for evening wear. As to shape, a chemise for sale in 1907 had a low-cut neckline with thin straps off the shoulder which could be replaced by ribbons or buttons, while from 1908, a square neckline was popular, the top of the chemise being trimmed with a lace and ribbon insert.

By 1900, the chemise was at calf- rather than knee length as previously; by 1914, it was well above the knee, revealing the drawers. There seems to have been a relationship between the length of the chemise and the height of the opening in open drawers; when this closed the chemise did not need to be so long – indeed it became little more than a vest, retained only by the older generation and worn by the young only in winter if at all.

Vests, Liberty Bodices and Camisoles

Vests and chemises seemed very similar by 1920 but vests were slimmer, briefer and more usually knitted than woven. They might be of silk or cotton or wool, perhaps ribbed, and had either an open 'French' or 'opera' neck or covered-in shoulders. In the 1920s, some vests had fancy tops with ribbon through the neck and at the armholes and in the 1930s, anything from a round neck with short or no sleeves, built-up shoulders or with straps. Some were waisted. The Shetland wool spencer of the 1930s had a V-neck, long sleeves and waist tie with basque. And in 1939, a three-quarter length knitted 'pettivest' appeared, to wear with panties.

Advertisement from the *Lady*, 6 November 1913. Chilprufe claimed that its pure wool underwear 'does not shrink, does not irritate, and does not get discoloured in the wash'.

A soft garment of fleecy-backed cotton reinforced with bands of tape, the liberty bodice fastened up the front with bone or rubber buttons, with extra buttons around the base to hold petticoats or suspenders. It was worn by young girls, replacing the uncomfortable and restrictive bodices they had worn before, and it remained popular from its introduction in 1908 throughout the Second World War into the 1950s.

In fabrics from cambric and nansook to silk ribbon, ninon and flannelette, the camisole served as a corset cover, or cache-corset, but it was later worn without a corset, and indeed sometimes, under a corset. In 1921, the *Tatler* carried an advertisement for camisoles in suede, stockinette, tricot, linen coutil (for sports) and satin coutil.

Usually fastened at the front with buttons, the camisole might be high at the neck with embroidery, lace and frills (tiers of starched frills added perhaps to enchance the bosom) or bare-necked with satin ribbons at the shoulder – or, rarely, no straps at all, held up by straps under the arms.

Page from a Gossard catalogue of the 1920s, showing the different styles of bra then available.

Brassières

As women turned from the upholstered look of the 1890s, the soft brassière appeared, often used in the early 1920s simply as a bosom flattener (in 1919, Sonia Keppel wore a 'broad band of satin ribbon' under her presentation dress when she went to Court) but by 1925 allowing for natural curves.

The word brassière did not immediately supersede all others. The terms bust extender, bust shaper and bust bodice were also in use around 1910. In America, from 1900, the term corset waist referred to a garment closer to a corset cover or camisole. Whatever the name used, these garments of cotton, linen, lace and ribbon were in fact all still based on the camisole until 1914, with just a little more structure, tightness and opacity. They were worn for decency and comfort as the corset receded downwards.

By 1910, brassières were available in cotton tricotrine, silk, satin; in 1920 *Vogue* advertised one in tulle; and in the 1930s sateen was particularly popular. Narrow, often ribbon, straps replaced built-up shoulders and the whole thing tended to be dainty and insubstantial – chiffon with black lace, brocaded satin and filet lace lined with silk, a far cry from the buckram of the bust bodice.

By the 1930s, the brassière was made to separate the breasts – there was a move to a shaped cup with the triangular Kestos style – and it was not long before the brassière was taking on the job of supporting and enchancing the breasts in the modern way.

Corsets

By the 1890s, the bustle had really had it day and was seen only on the old-fashioned in much abbreviated form with no more than a small pad supporting the skirt at centre back.

The corset was still heavily boned and laced, with a spoon busk to achieve a wasp waist; by 1900, it was straight-fronted and still a formidable structure, but by 1909-10 it had altered utterly as the natural slim up-and-down look came in. Corsets were long, low-fronted and back-laced tubes, becoming shorter again about 1914 and less heavily boned (there had been short 'sports' corsets for some years, often with elastic inserts for comfort), encouraged by the tango craze of the First World War years. Some corsets were no more than belts made out of strips of ribboning.

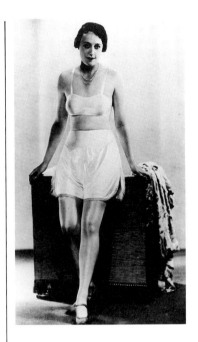

Gossard 1930s bra. An early example of separate bra and French knickers.

Kestos Advertisement, 1935. Kestos bra showing crossed straps feature at the back.

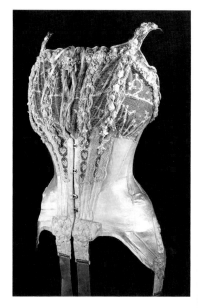

Wedding corset, 1905.
This white satin wedding corset, delicately embroidered with orange blossom, demonstrates how the corset has moved well below the bust with a piece of lace covering the shortfall, in anticipation of the brassiere.

Gossard catalogue, 1926. Four examples of long line corsets.

Light, unrestrictive foundation garments, often incorporating woven elastic, were popular in the 1920s – even the name corset was rejected in favour of belt or girdle – and by the 1930s, the elastic roll-on reigned supreme. Lace-up corsets were left to older women though they continued in production for many years.

The Corselette

A new garment called a corset brassière or corset bandeau developed in the United States from 1921. It combined the functions of the separate corset and the still new brassière and was more popularly called a corselette by 1926. It demonstrated a new use of woven elastic material and had its origins in an American 'slip on' in 1913 – then a dance corset with elastic inserts worn for the 1911-14 tango craze as well as the Charleston, Turkey Trot, Bunny Hug and other energetic dances. The first skating girdle, made by an American firm, Treo, in 1915, appeared with elastic and no lacing. There had also been a brassière-corset and knickerbocker-drawers combination (an all-in-one crêpe de Chine garment) on sale in Paris in 1914 for $50.

Other new arrivals in corsetry were the zip (early 1930s), spiral boning (1938) and, in 1935, the pantie-girdle or pantee-corset, also in two-way stretch elastic.

Corsets were mostly white, with coloured ribbons run through, and sometimes coloured; one from the 1890s is described as brocaded with flower sprays in bright colours such as blue and gold on black. In 1901, broché, silk batiste and coutil were available in white or blue and white, while in about 1910 corsets in drab, white and dove and French grey coutil were on sale. *Vogue* in 1917 advertised corsets, scantily boned, in figured silk and satin, while a 1921 *Tatler* article speaks of corsets of 'suede, stockinette, satin coutil, tricot and linen coutil'. Pastel colours were fashionable in the 1930s and in 1939 a 'nude' corset was advertised for sale.

From Drawers to Panties

At the beginning of the period, long drawers made of two full leg sections joined only at the back waist and fastening at the waist in front were still common. They might be of fine lawn, crêpe de Chine or silk, decorated with lace or ribbon, or of plain sensible flannel. An extant pair from 1905 are in black satin with tiny tucks at the back waistline and lots of lace and frilling to trim the legs – but by then they were more usually known as knickers and slightly less voluminous though still very full by modern standards. The between-the-leg opening began to be closed in the pre-World War I years though older people continued to prefer them open.

Patterns of 1906-8 for knickers suggested using calico, long-cloth, twill, flannel or flannelette. There were even patterns for knitting them in garter stitch!

In the same period, skirt knickers came in. Buttoned between the legs, these foreshadowed the later wide French knickers and camiknickers of the 1920s and 1930s. Directoire knickers appeared about 1909 – slim-fitting and closed with elastic at waist and knees, and these became immensely popular in knitted rayon (locknit), especially in the 1930s and 1940s.

As drawers became knickers so, in the 1920s, these 'knicks' became gradually shorter and shorter until they were the 'pants' or 'panties' of the 1930s.

Combinations

Combining chemise or camisole and drawers, combinations originated in 1877 and by the twentieth century were made in many forms and fabrics, long-sleeved and high-necked in wool for winter or in cotton with short or no sleeves for warm weather. Muslin, silk and lawn, trimmed with lace and decorated with embroidery, were also used. In 1900, Gwen Raverat referred to thick wool combinations worn under a white cotton pair with plenty of buttons and frills, while the Victoria & Albert Museum in London has a pair from 1905, of fine black silk threaded through with pink ribbon and trimmed profusely with lace.

Good for reducing bulk under the new slimmer fashions, for warmth and decency for women engaging in sporting activities, combinations proved an enduring favourite. For access, they were often left open at the inside leg, with buttons attached. Some knitted types would have no more than a discreet slit underneath.

Camiknickers

Introduced about 1916 and enjoying greatest popularity in the 1920s and 1930s, the camiknicker was essentially a shortened

Advertisement for Holmes & Co. Union undergarments, 1892. The American union underwear was known as combinations in England.

Advertisment for Pesco Underwear, 7 March 1911. Men's vests, drawers and combinations were popular in the 1880s and were still being worn by the 1930s.

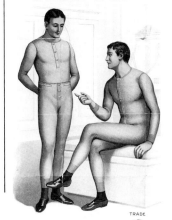

princess petticoat joined between the legs to some degree with a gusset on step-in models or a buttoned flap on others. Most were full at the leg, the length of which might vary from hip to mid-thigh, but some were gathered in a bloomer effect. Also of this era were cami-shorts, the shorts part buttoning up the sides. From 1927, camiknickers, shorter than ever, were scalloped over the hips.

Every sort of lightweight fabric was used for camiknickers including Milanese silk, lawn, and crêpe de Chine with ribbons, broderie anglaise and lace as decoration. Plain silk or sateen cut on the cross was popular in the 1930s. They came 'in all colours'.

Stockings, Garters and Suspenders

Unlike the lingerie, stockings were usually either black for winter or white for summer though they might be coloured to go with a dress, especially for evening wear. With the exposure of the legs in the 1920s, however, women wanted stockings in 'flesh' colours and a variety of pink, beige and fawn shades was manufactured in the recently introduced rayon, as well as in

Marlene Dietrich in The Blue Angel, 1930. Exploiting the image of temptress to manipulate men's fantasies, a version of power dressing.

Anny Ondra in
***Blackmail*, 1929.** An
early pair of
camiknickers featured in
the first British 'talkie'.

Advertisement from *Commerce and Industry*, 1931. How to wear one's singlet vest and drawers with style.

Children's waists (corsets) from the Gossard catalogue, 1926. The Gossard 'Athletic Waist' for boys, and 'Elfin Waist' for girls.

pure silk for best or for the better-off. Wool and cotton were also still worn but the real growth area was in rayon, from the first clumsy tubes to the fully fashioned styles of the next decade. Nylon stockings first made their appearance in America in 1938 but were not widely available in the UK until the early 1950s.

Stockings were usually attached to a suspender belt, which might be no more than a band of ribbon, or to suspenders on corsets or directly on brassières (where a corset was not worn). Garters were not totally superseded however (the suspender belt came in in 1887) – the 1920s saw pretty ruched garters with ribbon rosettes showing beneath the new short skirts.

Men

Men's shirts appeared in sizes from 14½ to 17 inches by 1909. The T-shirt came into existence, originally as an item of men's underwear in America. Men also wore combinations, all-in-one garments also known as union or combination suits. Pants reaching from waist to ankle were long johns in colloquial parlance. In the United States, boxer shorts were issued to infantrymen for summer wear in the First World War and were so comfortable that the soldiers retained them when they returned home as comfortable underwear. It was during this period also that Jockey patented the Y front. Construction briefs, a relation of boxer shorts, were introduced on 19 January 1935 in Chicago. A Marshall & Field Co. store sold 30,000 pairs in three months.[2] Men wore socks with suspenders right up to the Second World War.

Children's Underwear

Girls wore liberty bodices, knitted vests – sleeveless with ribbon threaded through at the neck – and knickers with elastic through holes at the waist or knicker frocks as advertised in *Good Housekeeping* in 1923, in wool knit or wool stockinette.

Boys wore short-sleeved vests buttoned at the neck and knickers, which became underpants at some point towards the 1950s. Most ready-made undergarments for children allowed for some modification as the children grew, for example camisoles had tabs to let out.

9

1890–1940: Making, Wearing and the Industry

Getting Dressed and Undressed

Before the First World War, getting dressed was itself a lengthy business, not only for the fashionable of the upper classes; a respectable woman might well wear warm woollen drawers under a decorative embroidered cotton pair, covered in turn by flannel then cotton petticoats. In Vita Sackville-West's *The Edwardians*, Viola watched her mother being dressed by her maid, who carefully drew on her silk stockings, fitted and adjusted her 'long stays of pink coutil, heavily boned' over her chemise, fastening the front busk, and then clipped her suspenders to her stockings. 'Then the lacing would follow, beginning at the waist and travelling gradually up and down, until the necessary proportions had been achieved.' Then there were 'pads of pink satin . . . fastened into place on the hips and under the arms, still further to accentuate the smallness of the waist', drawers, and then the petticoat 'spread into a ring on the floor' for her to step into.[1] Many poorer people, however, slept in the same underclothes they wore during the day, and there are numerous stories of children sewn into their underclothes for the winter, while in less affluent households men might have no more than a removable calico lining to their trousers, washed once a week and then sewn back in again.

But the younger generation was beginning to protest against the bulk of their underwear and particularly against uncomfortable corsets. Naomi Mitchison remembers in 1913 'an attempt, when I was sixteen, to put me into a laced corset, an unattractive contraption of heavy white cotton, whale-boned. But I firmly

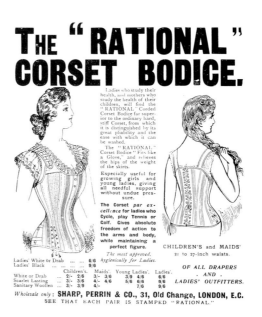

THE "RATIONAL" CORSET BODICE.

Ladies who study their health, and mothers who study the health of their children, will find the "RATIONAL" Corded Corset Bodice far superior to the ordinary hard, stiff Corset, from which it is distinguished by its great pliability and the ease with which it can be washed.

The "RATIONAL" Corset Bodice "Fits like a Glove," and relieves the hips of the weight of the skirts.

Especially useful for growing girls and young ladies, giving all needful support without undue pressure.

The Corset par excellence for ladies who Cycle, play Tennis or Golf. Gives absolute freedom of action to the arms and body, while maintaining a perfect figure.

The most approved hygienically for Ladies.

CHILDREN'S and MAIDS' 21 to 27-inch waists.

| | Ladies' White or Drab | ... ... | 6/6 |
| | Ladies' Black | ... ... | 9/6 |

	Children's.	Maids'.	Young Ladies'.	Ladies'.
White or Drab	2/- 2/6	3/- 3/6	3/9 4/6	6/6
Scarlet Lasting	3/- 3/6	4/- 4/6	5/6 6/6	9/6
Sanitary Woollen	3/- 3/9	4/- 4/-	7/6	9/6

Wholesale only: **SHARP, PERRIN & CO., 31, Old Change, LONDON, E.C.**
SEE THAT EACH PAIR IS STAMPED "RATIONAL."

Advertisement for the Rational Corset Bodice from the *Ladies' Field*, June 14 1902. For the sporting young lady, it was claimed that the Rational Corset Bodice was pliable and easy to wash, fastening with laces, buttons and possessing a busk at the centre only.

LES ÉPAULETTES "LAVASOUPLE"

LA CEINTURE "LAVASOUPLE"

LES JARRETELLES "LAVASOUPLE"

LA PETITE CEINTURE "LAVASOUPLE"

le Nouveau tissu élastique

LAVASOUPLE

TISSÉ FILÉS *Lastex*

élégant, très mince et résistant

se lave, se repasse comme le linge !

et ceci... est une fabrication **L'Extra Souple**

EN VENTE DANS LES GRANDS MAGASINS ET LES BONNES MAISONS

Advertisement for Lavasouple, 1934. These camiknickers possessed an integral belt, for ease of dressing and undressing, in the new material, lastex.

said it stopped me breathing when the waistline was pulled in, so that was given up and the whole thing came around my knees.' There was a move away from really restrictive corsets generally – women war workers were advised to wear them soft and easy-fitting – but even into the 1930s it was still not quite acceptable for a lady to go without her stays, though the boneless versions adopted by then were far from the fearsome constructions of their mothers. Ladies still wore what seems to us to be a lot of underwear but it had become far lighter and prettier than before.

Children – Clean and Snug

Even more than adults, children expected to wear layers of underclothes 'to aid healthy growth' as well as to keep out the cold. Alice Pollock remembers her schoolroom days in the 1890s wearing 'a flannel vest, cotton chemise, a bodice of buckram, on which buttons were sewn for cotton drawers to be buttoned on, a flannel petticoat sewn on to a bodice, and a cotton petticoat with a bodice.'[2] Wool was often worn next to the skin in accordance with the strictures of Dr Jaeger's sanitary underwear scheme of the 1880s. Substantial underwear remained a constant for schoolgirls for many years, especially heavy knickers in which not only hankies (routinely) but also when necessary purloined items or midnight feasts might be concealed and transported!

The problem of keeping all this thick intimate wear fresh was sometimes solved by the use of linings, for instance to serge knickers, which could be removed for laundering.

Making, Washing and Mending

Much lingerie was still hand-made – typically for a society lady, 'from Paris, mostly made from triple ninon appliquéd by French seamstresses'[3] or sewn by her maid. Most was made at home for personal use. There was also a big market, especially after the First World War, for companies providing patterns for everything from crochet yokes for camisoles to the popular sets of knickers, nightdress and chemise of the 1920s and 1930s. Also, fabrics could be bought ready-trimmed for making up at home. Harrods, in 1917, advertised an 'unmade camisole of embroidered jaconet (thick cotton cloth) 2s 11½d each'.

A weekly wash was the norm by the end of the nineteenth century. In 1892, Baroness Staffe wrote that a woman with good taste 'prefers comparatively simple underlinen, which there is no fear of washing, and which can be changed daily'. By then washing machines were being introduced into the big country houses while the middle classes had electric washers from the 1920s. Unless done by hand, however, washing of fine fabrics could be hazardous. Silks required special care while frayed lace, pin tucks coming unstitched, and embroidery losing its colour were all problems.

By the 1920s, block blue and a mixture of bicarbonate of soda and glucose were used to gain snowy white linen. Cheaper versions were made by colouring starch blue and adding gum arabic. Men's shirts would have required starching after each wash up to the Second World War and the whole wash would have had to be carefully ironed, especially the frills of the early years of the period, which required special goffering irons and hours of labour.

To avoid too much washing and to protect clothes from the smells and damaging effects of underarm perspiration, there were various devices which developed, from the perfumed sachets attached to dresses in the late nineteenth century. These might take the form of a sort of bodice or more usually of a pad, fastened to the dress under the arm with press studs. Similar corset shields and linings were also available.

Photograph of the Queen Mother, *c*1928-1930. A child unknowingly reveals her frilly knickers in the presence of the Queen Mother.

The Bachelor's Washing Day, coloured postcard, 1909. An early comic postcard depicting long-johns and shirts in the washing tub.

Sporting group of men, c1908. Good examples of the simple vests and trunks worn by most men around this era, especially when taking exercise.

Corsets were usually returned to the makers for repair so that bones, elastic, suspenders and clasps could be replaced and seams resewn – corsets took a lot of punishment. However, although many corsets were now washable, they often arrived in a very poor state and needed to be sprinkled with 'a solution of carbolic' and hung up to dry before work could begin. That this was a not uncommon problem may be seen from a declaration from the famous corset firm Spirella in 1935: 'Although it is preferred that garments are laundered before receipt, provision is made for this necessary work, as no used garment is allowed unlaundered into the workroom.'

As for home mending, there was always plenty of that. Careful darns were made in fine silk camiknickers, as in woollen vests and socks. Lingerie ribbon and mother-of-pearl buttons were a familiar aspect of haberdashery for underwear and needed constant replacing as they were worn out or lost. Liberty bodices were known for the propensity of their buttons to pop off at awkward moments: 'it usually flew off in Assembly during prayers and would leap from your leg and shoot across the hall to much stifled merriment and mirth from onlookers.'[4] School-girls might be expected to cope with these repairs themselves and also with the darning of their stockings. Runs in stockings were neatly mended with special silks. Lisle stockings were darned. This was not of course possible with the new sheer stockings of silk or rayon. Children's underwear was patched and darned repeatedly.

Stripes in underwear . . . starring Arrow Shorts with the Seamless Crotch. No irritating seam in the middle to cut you. 65¢ up. Undershirts 50¢ up.

Arrow Advertisement, 1935. Stripes were popular in the 1930s for men's underwear.

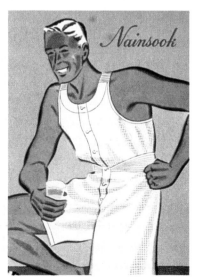

'Air cooled fabrics' from the American company BVD, 1935. It was claimed that they let the body breathe, and were similar to Aertex.

Spirella catalogue, 1926. Hip-retaining long-line brassière for the shapeless boyish silhouette required in the 1920s.

Buying and Selling

This was a time of expansion in the fields of advertising and marketing generally. The retail advertising of corsetry alone was a $1 million industry in the United States by 1914 though illustrations were initially restricted to line drawings, supplemented after 1932 by colour photos.

The big department stores in particular offered the opportunity to view a huge range of goods with the added advantage of excellent service. Not for nothing did D. H. Evans advertise itself in *The Ladies Field* of 1902 as having 'The largest Departments in the United Kingdom for Ladies' and Children's Outfitting' and claim to be 'Pioneers of the Renowned Irish Peasant Hand-Made underclothing Industries' and 'Originators of the Great White Sales and Shows'. A lady could visit a department store for a mannequin parade of corsetry and other underwear and have a fitting on the spot, her purchases being delivered later in one of the special long stay boxes, or she could make use of their mail order service. Some stores would send lingerie on approval to regular customers and Liberty's were known for their order service – 'in any colour or design desired' – for such items as hand-embroidered crêpe de Chine camiknickers.

The stores sold fabrics and haberdashery as well as half-made-up undergarments for finishing at home, but the real growth was in the ready-to-wear field as mass-produced machine-made lingerie became more acceptable in the early 1930s (particularly with the economic depression of these years).

The Industry

Warner Bros., the big underwear company, brought in rust-proof corsets in about 1900 after their founder pioneered a type of spring steel which was flat and coated against rust. The success of Spirella was also founded, in 1909, on an innovation, the new spiral steel which 'bends in all directions'.

An area of considerable expansion was in elastic materials after the development in about 1930, by the Dunlop Rubber Company, of elastic thread. In 1934, lastex batiste, hand-knitted elastic and chiffon lastex yarn are all mentioned in catalogues kept by the manufacturing company Berlei, followed in 1935 by satin lastex, French lastex-yarn lace and aeroknit elastic panels – and so on to woven elastics in 1939. Elastic was the really revolutionary element in underwear in this period.

But not only were there new inventions which benefited the industry and the customer, there was also a new attitude to the whole business of corset fitting – the corset had to fit the customer rather than the other way round! The better corsets were made to measure, with specialist firms developing and expanding their service of corsetières into people's homes. Gossard employed an all-woman staff so that customers could feel quite at ease.

Advertisement for A La Persephone from the *Ladies' Field*, 1902. Art Nouveau-style advertising was all the rage in the early 1900s, here illustrating a straight-fronted corset, cut low on the bust, with four attached suspenders.

Advertisement for Weingarten Bros. from the *Ladies' Field*, June 14 1902. The S Bend, as shown here, distorted the spine, compressing the waist and abdomen.

Advertisement for Bon Ton and Royal Worcester Kidfitting Corsets, c1913. Maternity corsets, corsets designed for comfort and expansion, they had six suspenders and side gussets of elastic, well below the bosom.

VISITORS TO LONDON who seek to be corseted in the very latest mode are cordially invited to avail themselves of the services of our Expert Fitters in order to assure that latest touch which gives the outer garments their character and distinctiveness. A fitter will be sent to your hotel with a selection of the celebrated Bon Ton or Royal Worcester Kidfitting Corsets upon request by telephone or post.

AMERICAN LADIES will find in our Corset Showrooms a full range of the newest models of Bon Ton Corsets, which are, by special arrangement, shown here simultaneously with the first exhibits in New York, Paris and Vienna.

PETER ROBINSON'S, OXFORD STREET. LONDON, W.

Telephone: GERRARD 8512.

Gossard Catalogue, 1928. Pink long-line Gossard corset (*insert right*).

Flapper and Friend from *La Vie Parisienne* c1920. The new dances of the 1920s required underwear that would allow for energetic movement. Long-line corsets were worn to obtain the boyish straight-hipped look (*right*).

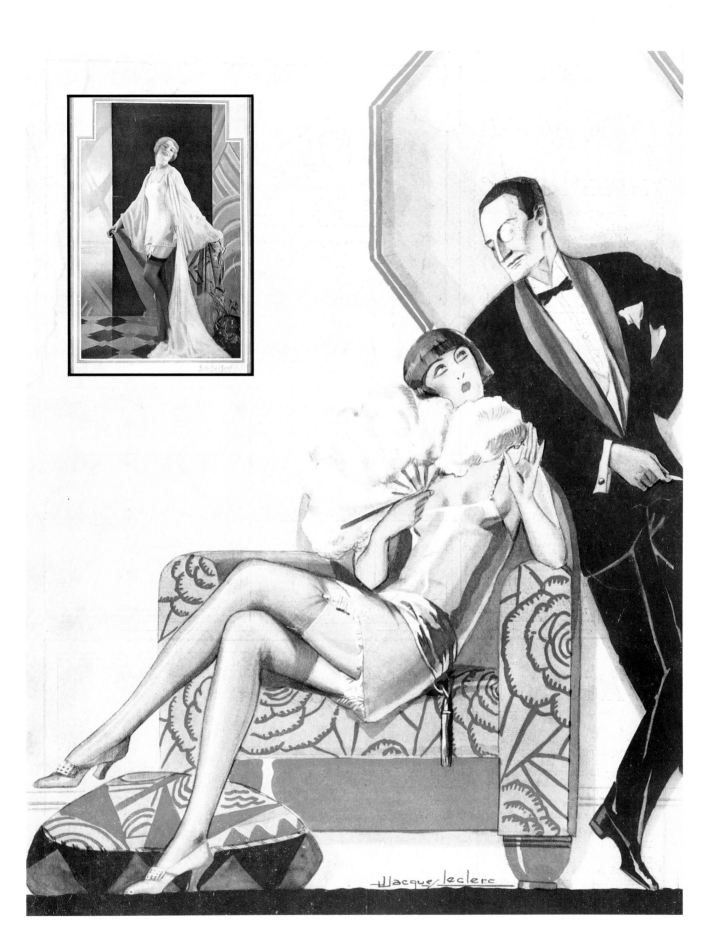

Jacque leclerc

Knitwear was still important in underwear and its British manufacture centred on Leicester, Nottingham and on factories in Scotland; Scottish knitwear was in great demand between the wars and the trade-names and names of designs bear this out – 'Braemar,' 'Balmoral' and 'Kelvin' are just a few.

The underwear trade began to organize itself internally as it expanded and became more sophisticated. 1901 saw the launching of *Les Dessous Elégants*, the first trade journal to be devoted exclusively to underwear, and in 1907 the Corset Manufacturers Association of the United States was founded (by 1938 known as the Corset and Brassière Association of America). In 1913, the *American Corset and Underwear Review* was founded, for buyers of corsets and brassieres, to offer information, 'fashion forecasts, market reports, store economics, business management and current news'. By this time the wholesale industry had a $40 million turnover volume.

Spirella factory floor, 1910. The Spirella factory was opened in Letchworth in 1909, having initiated spiral steels in 1904. The workforce consisted entirely of women.

10

1940–90: Outside In: The Silhouette

The concept of feminine beauty and the ideal figure shape changed considerably in this period. There were ever more energetic health cults: exercise and diet, tennis and walking in the 1950s and especially in the 1960s and 1970s through to yoga, swim fitness courses, jazz dance and stretch classes, aerobics and callanetics in the 1980s and '90s. Woman's image of herself changed with her new independence, self-reliance and financial freedom.

The Second World War

The war presents a major hiatus in the history of twentieth-century corsetry and underwear fashions. For a start it was extremely difficult to get hold of supplies at all for British women. Corsetry factories were set to making goods for the British armed services. Also, many materials normally used in corsetry manufacture were needed for the war effort. Cotton imported (with difficulty) from the United States, Egypt and India rose in price and was in short supply in America as in Britain. In America, silk was used for powder bags, gas bags and parachutes. Steel was naturally very scarce and recycling of corset bones, especially those of steel, was practised.

The Malayan rubber plantations fell to Japan in 1941 and an American government edict cut rubber production by 50 per cent. Synthetic rubber was in limited production for military needs only, for gas masks and other military equipment. In America, foundation wear finishing tape was used for cartridge belts and brass armaments manufacture took over from production of hooks, eyes and stocking supporters. Lace machines were even employed to make camouflage nets. Nylon, invented around

Illustration by David Wright from the *Sketch*, **1942.** World War II continued its influence on advertising with these black camiknickers in silk or rayon satin.

Culotte Velo-Ski from Silhouette, 1946. How easy it is to get skirts hitched up in knicker elastic!

Healthguard advertisement, 1950. Nylon stockings were becoming increasingly refined by 1950 *opposite*.

1938, was used in parachutes and glider tow-ropes, preventing its use for underwear until about 1947. The first nylon stockings did not go on sale in Britain until 1946, though some lucky women obtained them from American GIs well before this.

The styles of the early 1940s were square-shouldered with straight or frugally pleated skirts to just below the knee. Trousers, dungarees and boiler suits were all adopted by women, first for work and then for leisure. Because of the war and rationing there was a general economy of fabric used in clothing. No extravagance or wastefulness was allowed.

Culotte "Velo-Ski"

MADOR
32 et 34, RUE DES JEUNEURS
PARIS

EST INDISPENSABLE AUX SPORTIVES ÉLÉGANTES

Sweet and lovely in...

Healthguard

...woollies

lovelier still in Vayle Scottish nylons by John Skelton

Figure Precautions

Advertisement for Berlei from *Vogue*, October 1941. 'Controlette' foundation with suspenders and stockings.

Jane Russell in *The Outlaw*, 1943. The high-profile image was achieved by wearing an uplift bra.

Rationing

Underwear, like all clothing, came under the rationing restrictions through the Utility scheme introduced in 1941. What was produced was actually of high quality. Cotton vests and knickers and men's underpants were particularly praised although the corsets and stockings were not. No metal or elastic was used in these government-restricted designs. American women had 'L-90' bras and girdles from 1942, the equivalent of Utility underwear in Britain.

All-in-one garments were popular as not only were they cheap and easy to wear but they were low on coupons.

Gossard bra, 1940s.
This bra from the 1940s
features circle-stitching
on the cups with an
elastic net girdle and
rigid brocade front.

Utility underwear,
*c*1941. Knitted vests and
pants in styles which
persist today.

Morale and Morals

Wartime propaganda and nationalistic feeling were reflected in the advertising of the time. Berlei launched a series of eye-catching advertisements to remind its erstwhile customers of its continued existence, despite rationing and shortages, and pointed up its own war efforts. Meanwhile women knitted sensible, comfortable woollen underwear – vests and body belts – for servicemen.

Underwear was used during the war to display national flags and colours, for instance the bulldog with Union Jack seen on Utility camiknickers. Posters of women in their undies were used to maintain morale amongst the troops, and the trend to uplift in brassières (which had been developing for some ten years before the war) was possibly seen as a symbolic reflection of moral uprightness to help maintain a positive attitude and self-belief!

English Rose advertisement, 1950. The flower of modern foundations, corsetry model shop window display piece showing brassiere and corset.

Pantie-girdle and body controllers, Triumph, c1960s.

The 1930s had seen the development of free and easy attitudes towards display of the female form and this had been seen in the various states of undress which were allowed in print and in advertising as well as in film publicity stills. They were not, however, allowed in the movies. The Hays censorship code reigned in Hollywood from 1922 to 1945. Ironically, one rule, strictly promulgated, regarding dresses cut low in front led to the appearance of sexy backless dresses as film makers introduced Victorian-style underwear into their Westerns to create interest. However, they sometimes went too far: the metallic bra designed for Jane Russell to wear in the Western *The Outlaw*, made in 1943, succeeded in keeping the film off the screens for six years for reasons of morality.

SHAPE UP WITH *St Michael®*

Figure-watchers, don't despair! You can shape up with St Michael bras, girdles and corselettes and get the curves in the right places. Foundation garments like these give you a shape to be proud of.

From left to right: pale lemon stretch bra, 13s 11d, with matching tricot medium control, brief leg, pantee girdle, 19s 11d; firm control pantee corselette, 69s; vivid print nylon bra, 11s 11d; firm control pantee girdle, 27s 11d; medium control pantee corselette, 58s; stretch bra with padded under-cup and stretch straps, 17s 11d; firm control short leg pantee girdle in nylon and Lycra stretch lace, 37s 6d.

Post-War Designer Lingerie

The corset returned in France in 1946 with a waist cincher by Robert Piguet and Marcel Rochas's *guêpière*, a belt which 'strangled' the waist. Christian Dior's New Look of 1947 saw a complete revival of the hour-glass figure, a pinched-in waist contrasted with full ballerina-length skirt and well-emphasized bust. Bustiers designed by Rochas in 1943 and Jacques Fath in 1946 had prepared the way for this silhouette which was to dominate fashions in the 1950s.

The new fashionable lingerie being advertised, such as designer Molyneux's delicious floral-printed white chiffon chemise with brassière top in the *Harper's Bazaar* for March 1947, was scarce and expensive and most women had to adapt what they already had. The immediate post-war years were hard with rationing remaining in force until 1951 and some restrictions on corsetry until 1955. However, the home-dressmaking fashions of 1946 in Paris and 1947 in London were quick to take up the new tailored look, in slips with darted bust, a shaped waist with yoke, and a fuller, six-gored skirt. As soon as material could be found the new styles were adopted.

PANTS REVOLUTION: his and hers

The revolution's here! Underwear for men and girls has never been so colourful. 1970 styles are definitely much more brief, clingy and fashion conscious than ever before.

1950s – New Look, New Freedom?

The new line encouraged extravagance. Even before the war Marshall & Snelgrove were selling hooped petticoats for crinoline-effect skirts as seen on Queen Elizabeth (the Queen Mother) in her Norman Hartnell imitation of the Worth dresses worn by European princesses in the middle of the nineteenth century. The 1939 film, *Gone with the Wind* led to a surge in demand for extravagant crinolines, once the war was over. A Pierre Balmain dress in *Vogue* April 1952, is described as 'Black penny spots on white chiffon over a crinoline of palest pink tulle, the hip swathing knotted into a soft bustle.'

Not many could afford a Balmain but everyone was determined to have a full skirt: hips were padded out with foam rubber and embellished with ruffles, while in 1950, paper nylon petticoats served to kick out skirts for parties and dancing. Flocked ninon nylon was all the rage as were frou-frou petticoats with layers of stiffened net and frills. Full-skirted petticoats survived until about 1957 when slim skirts and sheath dresses demanded straight slips again. The A-line, which came in about

Advertisement for Sidroy from *Drapers Record*, March 15, 1958. The sweater is worn over a pointed spiral stitched bra, with waist slip and high-cut pants with side ruching.

Lana Turner wearing a slinky black body suit in the 1950s.

1957, rivalled but never outshone the New Look shape, although the latter was really better suited to the average English or American woman's shape!

In August 1950, the revival of strapless dresses led to a renewed demand for strapless boned undergarments and there was a craze for strapless brassières and corselettes. A sort of caved-in look developed, epitomized by Warner's 'Merry Widow' waspie of 1951 – strapless, waisted with a boned curved back and long suspenders.

There were even evening and cocktail dresses with integral corsetry, a boned bodice or 'built-in brassière'. Busts were pushed up with padding if necessary. The American word 'cleavage' came into its own. In 1953, Berlei brought out a Hollywood Maxwell brassière, the original 'whirlpool' brassière – favourite of film stars – in nylon or cotton batiste and net. It came in pink, white or black, with 'continuous stitching moulds, full, perfectly rounded contours . . . defined separation and the newest "forward" look'. The 'sweater girl' era peaked in 1957 with tight-fitting jumpers worn by day and plunging necklines by night. Lana Turner was just one of a succession of film stars who flaunted generous busts at this time. In 1953, Triumph brought out a bra which was circular stitched and cone shaped to give what was known as the Brigitte Bardot look. Jayne Mansfield and Marilyn Monroe (who wore Spirella) were two others who particularly influenced the appearance of women's busts in the 1950s.

New Freedoms

Advertising laws were more relaxed from the mid 1950s and it was possible to advertise underwear on the television for the first time. This helped to revive the industry and broke the taboo on discussion of the subject. A whole new art form developed around the portrayal of underwear in films and on television, in advertising, in photography and magazine illustrations and in slogans. It was a film that launched the nightwear fashion known, still, as the 'Baby Doll', a short nightgown with matching brief puff panties beneath.[1] In the film, Carroll Baker appeared in just such an outfit and that was enough for it to become the rage.

Television was a powerful influence. The US company Maidenform advertised on television in 1958 and in 1957 Berlei

Advertisement for Roussel, 1945/6. A French corset of the 1940s with spiral stitched shaping on the cups.

113

Elizabeth Taylor in *Cat on a Hot Tin Roof*, 1958. Elizabeth Taylor dressed in simple silk slip.

Brigitte Bardot in *Heaven Fell That Night*, 1957. Brigitte Bardot sporting a very 1990s looking black lace bodysuit.

became the first company in Britain to advertise on television and in national papers and magazines. *Vogue* and other glossy women's magazines were also highly influential in promoting an image of what the beautiful woman looked like (in her undergarments among others) and in general people became used to seeing more women, and men, in a state of what would earlier have been called *déshabille*!

Attitudes to sex (and prudery) were changing and women were pursuing more active lifestyles though they might still, in the 1950s especially, choose to devote themselves to home life. Not only were they free to wear the trousers, but also they freed themselves from most of the restrictive underwear previously considered essential for decency. The term bikini came in around 1946 and bikini-style briefs developed for both male and female. In general knickers gave way to closer cut panties and trunks or boxer shorts. When 'support' was worn it was in neatly cut light elastics.

The Teenage Market – A New Body of Opinion

By 1950, following the lead of the United States, teenagers were identified as a distinct market where previously children's or 'maids' fashions had sufficed. The needs of young girls for suitable and sympathetic underwear of their own were acknowledged and special ranges were introduced, such as the Lilies range for college girls by Lilies of France in America and the Teenform collection for pre-teens imported into Britain by Berlei.

1960s – Fraught Femininity

The celebrated mini was the hallmark of the decade, with fairly straight cut clothes in the late 60s. The sexual revolutionaries directly targeted underwear, that is, the bra, as the 'yoke of oppressive femininity' and rejected it utterly, though bra-burning was more symbolic than actual! It made good headlines though rather than go without one at all most young women chose bras that were either very lightweight or something like designer Rudi Gernreich's 'no-bra bra' which gave support while giving a 'nothing-under' effect. His 1965 range for Exquisite Form came in sheer tricot nylon in white, black, or most popular, nude, and even included a 'none-in-one corselette'.

The figure-hugging styles of the early 1970s left little to the imagination, but raised the problem of the 'visible panty line'. Outfit by Ossie Clark.

The waif-like skinny look initiated by Twiggy in the 1960s, required only the bare minimum of underwear.

In tune with the days of 'flower power' Emannuelle Khan in 1968 designed a lovely white tulle bra with strategically placed white lace flowers for Erys, while in 1969 Ungaro put his models into metal bras – a move towards the technological future perhaps? Body stockings (about 1965) were also used to get a smooth-all-over look as was the original Warners 'Birthday Suit' of 1961, a light pantie-corselette which used Lycra to create a seamless, close-fitting garment more like a swimsuit than anything else. Tights were a big innovation of the 1960s, pulled into fashion from sports and winter wear by the mini skirts of 1965-70.

1970s – Versatility

The 1970s saw a continuation of minimalist underwear beneath a constantly changing hemline with the midi-length skirt, hot pants, peasant dresses and flared trousers coming and going. There were tights with built-in panties, halter-neck bras (1972), the bodyshaper from Gossard, and the arrival of moulded undergarments – seamless, one-piece bras and panties, almost invisible in wear and very comfortable. There were even disposable paper pants on sale by 1973.

Clothes were often 'unisex', variety prevailed, and this was reflected in underclothes. There was also a revival of romanticism with soft 'Edwardian' lace-trimmed camisoles and frilly petticoats and even broderie anglaise bloomers, as well as a return, led by Janet Reger, to more glamorous fancy lingerie of every sort from silk French knickers to flimsy negligées and sexy suspender sets.

1980s – Flexibility

These years saw unprecedented variety and lack of conformity in fashion: there was no longer 'a' hemline for instance, women wore jeans or trousers as readily as mini skirts, and a 'little black corset' was acceptable evening wear in all but the stuffiest circles. The square-shouldered look of the 1940s reappeared with built-in shoulder pads and slim skirts as women 'power' dressed in the style of influential TV soap operas *Dallas* and *Dynasty*. The softer style of the 'caring' 1990s has seen a craze for loose-fitting tops and figure-hugging skirts and leggings. In

the same way, underwear to suit almost any taste and occasion could be found in the shops (hand-made was only for the very few). Whether you wanted lace-trim petticoats in ivory or shell-pink, delicately pleated French knickers or naughty red lace basques or even a sensible Vedonis vest, it was available. Women also began to wear boxer shorts, tanga briefs, body stockings and special sports bras.

Underwear was endorsed by famous names, in, for instance, advertisements for the Gap chain of shops, and also 'came out' as outerwear in the collections of Parisian designer Jean-Paul Gaultier (for example a 'Dervish' a bra of tasselled fez hats) and of Vivienne Westwood (the mini-crini of 1985-6). Madonna became famous in the mid-1980s wearing a form of corset as a stage costume and many ordinary women followed the trend in a much more moderate way, for instance wearing a silk camisole as an evening top.

Underwear-inspired outerwear, taken to an extreme by Paco Rabanne in 1971.

— 11 —

1940–90: Inside Out: Undergarments

In a trend initiated a century ago, matching sets have characterized the lingerie of the period, from the slip and panties of the 1950s to the camisole, slip and knickers, cropped top and tangas of the 1980s, and from the more traditional knitted 1930s-style vests and pants of mail order and chain stores to the trendy thermal vests and long-john pants of the ski-set. In the 1960s, bra and girdle were coordinated with colour- and design-matching underwear in different fabrics; in the 1970s, bras and briefs came in a more integrated mix-and-match range which included slip, half-slip and camisole, corselette or basque and suspender belt. The sophistication of stretch fabrics and the development of stretch laces and woven, knitted and Lycra fabrics all printed, brocaded or embroidered with the same design flourished in the 1980s, with camiknickers, teddies and bodies demonstrating some of the possibilities. Men's underwear has needed less coordination, usually comprising one item only, but where vests have been worn they have been coordinated with long johns, trunks, jockeys and briefs. Now a man can have boxer shorts and a tie to match!

Materials

The term 'underlinen' has become a complete anachronism for the underwear of the late twentieth century. Linen has remained an expensive fabric throughout the period. It has been almost exclusively used for smart outer-wear and sportswear, the problem of its creasing never satisfactorily overcome. During the war, cotton was off the market. Afterwards it returned in small quantities.

Plain cotton interlock knickers and vests for children and

120

Black lacy basque, 1991. Lightly boned, underwired basque, low cut for plunging necklines.

cotton lawn for girls' slips were advertised in the 1950s. The finer qualities of cotton became comparatively expensive, luxury fabrics. At the upper end of the market were cotton coutil corsets and cotton batiste bras (smoother and lighter weight with more give). Because of its cost, cotton was cast aside by the popular market in favour of cheaper artificial fibres which dominated from the 1950s through to the early 1970s: these were nylon and polyester under the trademark Terylene.

Cotton gussets to nylon pants were still employed in better quality production, for medical reasons, being less likely to foster bacteria than nylon. Cotton returned in force when combined with polyester in the late 1970s and became once again a staple of underwear in the 1980s, middle-class purists now being prepared to spend extra to obtain the healthy comfort of a natural fibre. Cotton and cotton Aertex remained popular with sports enthusiasts throughout, for vests and pants. Cotton string vests, introduced for men in the late 1940s, also held their own for some time for summer wear under cotton and polyester-cotton shirts.

Woollen underwear, both woven and knitted, was popular into the 1950s for children and men though it lost its importance as central heating was installed in homes throughout Europe, but it returned for winter sports wear in the 1980s. Mixed fibre underwear incorporating wool and nylon, combed cotton, cotton and nylon, orlon, banlon and other mixtures came on to the market in 1958.

During the restrictions of 1941-55 cotton sateen, rayon satin, rayon crêpe, Celanese rayon locknit, and wool were the usual Utility fabrics for underwear. From 1945, parachute silk (actually silk, rayon or nylon), slipper satin and nylon were available. By 1950, pure silk could be had but was expensive, so only for the few. Nylon and other man-made fibres were manufactured on a large scale from the 1950s. Nylon was non-absorbent but it could be woven so as to keep it porous. When it began to appear there was much interest in this exciting new material. It came in many forms such as machine-knitted nylon tricot (by 1949), nylon net, nylon marquisette (1951), nylon taffeta, voile and lace, nylon seersucker (as produced by the Adlis Bra Company in 1955) and even nylon broderie anglaise (as in the English Rose range of bras and girdles launched in the spring of 1955). A corselette named 'Sensation'

Marks & Spencer Fortuny pleat and lace bustier and French knickers, 1991. This classic but contemporary combination of luxurious pleating in a modern fabric has proved to be enormously successful.

Practical living, 1989.
The new sporty shapes
are apparent in these
combinations of cropped
tops and simple cotton
briefs.

had nylon satin front panels in 1952 and a Spirella bra of 1959
even had nylon jacquard.

Another man-made material was rayon, mixed with cotton for
example, to create a shiny rayon pattern on a cotton ground, or
even with nylon to increase its absorbency and warmth.

Polyester and acrylic were two further developments of the
1950s as was Terylene (from 1956) and last but not least Lycra

(1959). Lycra is the most important of a group of man-made elastics known originally as Spandex fibres or elastomerics and renamed elastane by the EEC in 1976. Containing no natural rubber at all Lycra is lighter and far more powerful than rubber elastic and has proved itself invaluable in foundationwear.

The 1960s saw wide use of Terylene and the introduction of nylon bones for corsetry, while in the 1970s silk retreated to the upper end of the market, leaving the lower end to nylon. Polycotton was popular but cotton was still expensive, though after 1983 there was a real return to pure cotton. At the end of the 1980s, Marks & Spencer brought out their top underwear range in jacquard satin, silk, silk damask and elastic lace. At a more sober level, they used polyviscose for their thermal wear.

Colour

Pastels, pale pinks, blues, yellows and greens were used for underwear in the 1940s. Women wanted to look pretty underneath even if wearing a uniform or sober Utility garb on top.

Tea-rose, skin-tone, pink and some brighter colours such as yellow were favoured in the 1950s. The *Drapers Record* noted that 1955 had seen the introduction of colour 'bursts of red, yellow and green among the white, pink and black in brassière selections and in lightweight belts and pantie-girdles'. Pink, however, by 1956, was 'no longer the power it was only a few years ago' (*Drapers Record* again) and even *Punch* of 16 March 1955 states 'Colours are black, white, mink and blue. There is no pink - not in Paris. For more than 30 years pink has been the accepted corset colour and for belt and brassieres.'

Just about every colour was popular in the 1960s. There was a lot of black and white but also bright shades from the Italian firm La Perla and lovely subtle tones such as ivory, crème caramel, champagne and tea-rose. Manufacturers also tried out more unusual colours, for example Berlei used navy blue in 1967, Tobago brown and Caribbean blue in 1968 and sky, jade and apple in 1969.

Printed fabrics, especially with floral motifs, were also widely used, for example Berlei's desert flower prints of spring 1969. However, by 1971, neutral tones had come back in as viscose and polycotton summer dresses were not always opaque and patterned underwear showed through. Berlei's flowers became skin-tone; pinks and pastels regained their sway.

'Bee Dees' by Triumph, 1990. Black and white check step-in cropped top and brief. Suitable for underwear or outerwear.

The fresh cotton underwear of the early 1980s looked good in bright colours but the later 1980s saw a preference for more subtle sophisticated shades. Some companies in particular were known for their unusual colours, for instance Charnos with its maroon, jade and navy and Warners whose spring 1991 catalogue included emerald and aubergine. In spite of this the majority of underwear in the 1980s was in white, black or a pastel shade – mostly pink or beige/coffee. There was a revival of prints in the late 1980s but they were far more delicately conceived, on silk-like polyester, than previously.

The Garments

Largely a garment of the past, the chemise still cropped up occasionally. Molyneux designed one as part of a collection in the early 1950s. In 1990, the name made something of a come-back referring to a long camisole – or short slip – in tailored woven fabric, rather than knitted as before. Vests were widely worn in the 1940s and 1950s but central heating and sexual revolution largely eliminated them except for little children and the old and for winter wear. So vests were mainly for warmth, in, for example, interlock knit, in blended wool, cotton and bri-nylon (by Wolsey) and in polyester (Marks & Spencer's 1990 thermal wear). Marks & Spencer also, in about 1967, brought in 'cosy tops' in stretch bri-nylon to appeal to the young who wouldn't have been seen dead in a vest but still felt the cold!

The camisole also experienced intermittent popularity with revivals in every decade but the swinging sixties. Usually with front buttons or ties but occasionally pulling over the head, the camisole refused to die – and even crossed the line into outwear in the 1980s.

Petticoats and Slips

Waist petticoat, waist skirt or half slip, the petticoat was an enduring standard. In the 1940s, the Utility version was straight and pleat-less to save on material and fell to just below the knee. With the full skirts of the New Look and the 1950s, frothy petticoats with nipped-in waists were in demand. Layers of stiffened net and frills might be required for evening or party wear. Petticoats with removable hoops were also used to obtain the desired full look.

By 1957, an alternative slim-line waist petticoat with a front inverted pleat was fashionable. Absolutely straight petticoats with a simple slit at centre front, side or centre back were also worn – one version, the 'espresso', being straight but with a froth of frills at the hem.

Cotton with broderie anglaise was very popular for petticoats as was paper nylon with Swiss embroidery. Petticoats usually fastened at the side waist with buttons or poppers; elasticated waists didn't come in until the 1960s. The 1980s saw embroidered and curved hems and also wrap-over styles.

The waist slip went up for the mini in the late 1960s and down to a wide bell shape for the knee-length skirts of the mid-1970s, and further down, to the ankle, for the ethnic look. By 1990, Marks & Spencer had waist petticoats in several different lengths all at one time, to cater for different heights and tastes. The 1940s' slips had more fullness at the bust and shaped corselets to the waist by 1946/7 in nylon ninon. Slips were quite tailored for the day, with gored panels. Fluted nylon or permanent pleating trim was popular around 1956 for the hem and bodice of slips and 1957-8 saw deep hem flounces with lace and ribbon insertions and edgings. By 1958, the slip was shorter and by 1968, very short – the bra slip of the mini-skirt era. By the early 1970s, there were full-length slips with bra cups and detachable straps but this was a relatively short-lived vogue. The fabrics in which slips and petticoats were made were constantly being improved on, especially artificial fibres such as nylon and polyester where the concern was particularly to achieve a cling-resistant, anti-static garment.

Knickers

The early 1940s saw camiknickers knitted in two-ply wool and fastened with ribbon and pearl buttons or cut with extreme economy from coupon-precious fabric. A 1949 model might have been shaped and darted at the waist, with a shaped corselet like the slip, with a fuller 'skirt' to go with the new outer styles. Washing satin was a popular fabric as was a fine knit in wool and rayon mixture. Camiknickers fell from favour for many years until revived in the 1980s in a variety of man-made, easy-care fabrics.

Bloomer drawers, gathered at waist and knee, were both warm and comfortable for war work. Knickers were full and wide-legged, buttoning at the side; they might be yoked in the later 1940s and were still popular in the 1950s in 30-denier nylon with a 15-denier flounce.

Panties or pantees were closer fitting with a shorter, cut-away leg. A 1944 style had a trimming of drawn thread work. Both knickers and panties might be set on a shaped waistband yoke in the late 1940s (like the slip). From 1949, knickers were available in nylon tricot.

Pants were still fairly 'covering' in the 1950s and 1960s. It was not until the 1970s and 1980s that really brief bikini-type pants were widespread and even then there were throw-backs, for example the fashion for demi-johns, above-the-knee stretch underpants in the late 1960s.

The tight hipsters and jeans of the 1970s led to pressure for hip- rather than waist-high pants to go with them and there was constant concern about a 'VPL' (visible panty line) with the tight jeans and skirts.

Briefs got even briefer in the mid-1980s with the 'high leg' cut but low leg panties were still available. There was something to suit everybody from tap pants and tanga briefs to culottes (culotte slips in nylon jersey or polycotton), boxer shorts in silk and voile, Sloggis in cotton and Lycra or thermal long johns. There were even disposable 'paper' pants of 78 per cent viscose and 22 per cent acetate.

The Bra

The bras of the 1940s and early 1950s tend to look fairly sensible to the modern eye, specially the long-line type with hook-and-eye front fastening. Even the supposedly glamorous strapless bra (sometimes with removable straps) of the 1950s was quite a sturdy item.

Progress had been made in sizing, with cup size being taken into account (generally A, B, C or D) as well as just the round-the-bust measurement, and there was a move to greater emphasis on the bust with criss-cross stitching to the bra cup for uplift by 1948. 'Whirlpool' or circular stitching was employed on the bra cup in the 1950s to create the requisite pointed 'cone' breasts of the era. Foam pads might also be inserted by 1940 to give a fuller bosom and in the 1950s many women found themselves resorting to 'falsies', 'cuties' or padded bras in order to achieve the correct profile.

'Nadja' by Triumph, 1990. Cropped cotton top with square neckline and floral lace insert. Brief has lace at the front and a wide waistband for comfort.

Bra, knickers and suspenders from the popular 'Gipsy' range by Berlei, from 1976 *opposite*.

Bra and French knickers and camiknickers, *c*1988. A modern feel is given to these camiknickers and bra and knickers, by use of a strong combination of colours and floaty light chiffon.

The 1950s' obsession with the bust also led to various plunge and strapless bras. Underwired cups were revived in 1945 and continued to be used in even quite dainty bras, especially where extra support or uplift was needed, for instance in 1960s' low-cup styles with lace or net front and wide-set straps. Over this period, however, modern developments, in stretch elastic fabrics particularly, meant that bras could be prettier, quite cut-away (even backless in 1983!) and still do their job. Very attractive half-cup or deep-plunge models in apparently flimsy fabrics were just as effective as the 'sensible' styles they replaced – if not more so, for instance the Gossard 'Wonderbra' launched in 1968.

Some popular fabrics used were: nylon lace-lined voile (late 1940s), mercerised poplin and broché (1947), superfine poplin, nylon and art silk (Exquisite Form 1957), lace and marquisette, in black and scarlet (also 1957), lace and net with underwiring (1964) on to the all man-made Triumph bra of 1988-9, 45 per cent nylon, 45 per cent polyester and 10 per cent elastane. Even Marks & Spencer's 'Victorian lace collection' of 1990 used all man-made fabrics.

Berlei catalogue, 1971. Sales assistant's guide to measuring customers for a bra.

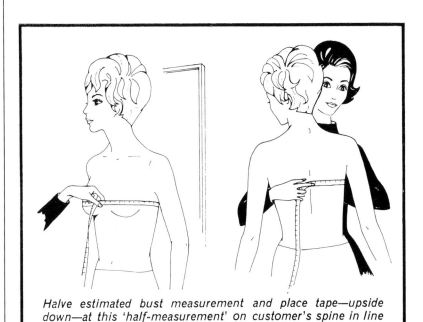

Halve estimated bust measurement and place tape—upside down—at this 'half-measurement' on customer's spine in line with mid-root of bust. Bring ends round through mid-root and over the nipple, taking the measurement between the breasts. Check in mirror that tape is in correct position on the back.

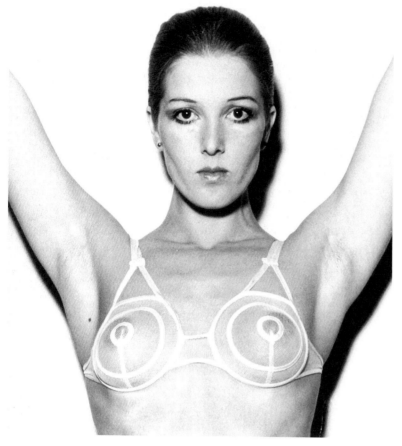

Sizing became more refined also in the post-war years with everything from AA through to DD sizes commonly available and even FF from Berlei. Some companies in particular specialised in larger sizes, for instance Fantasie Foundations who sold sizes E to G. But there was also a venture into a type of bra where exact fit was less important – if comfort even more important – the sports bra in all-stretch fabric which was simply put on over the head and eased into, adapting automatically to the wearer's shape.

Corsets, Corselettes, Girdles, Pantie-Girdles

The traditional stiffened corset had really had its day by 1940 but older women continued to wear it, for many years sometimes, and it still continues in production – just. It might be either laced or elasticated and was worn by this time next to the skin, rather than over a vest or chemise as before.

**Leggings and corset,
1990.** Leggings gain new
stylishness, when teamed
with a short, soft corset
in pure white cotton.

**Layal bodyshaper,
1991/2** *left*.

**Janet Reger basque
and wrap,** *c* **late 1980s.**
Janet Reger has been
producing covetable
underwear since the
early '70s *opposite*.

135

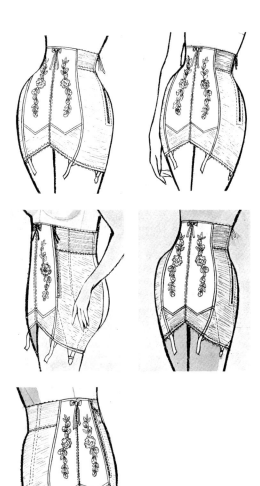

Berlei catalogue, 1966.
The Berlei five figure –
types for 'gay Slant'
range of corselettes

Berlei Catalogue, 1971.
Light, medium and firm
control pantees, girdles
and 'gay Slant'
corselettes from Berlei.

The girdle took over the job of control for most women – elasticated, and either side-hooking, semi step-in or busk-fronted, it remained a firm favourite. However, the roll-on gained ground, with two-way stretch elastic giving extra control without extra weight after 1960, and the corselette was also very popular through the 1960s and 1970s.

Women of the post-war years could in fact choose from a wide variety of foundation garments – including also the pantie-corselette and pantie-girdle – just the combination of cover and control they wanted. They might want something fairly powerful but below the waist only, or a light, smoothing garment from bust down to thighs. Modern technological developments meant there was something to suit everyone, the moulded pantie-girdle of the late 1970s being one of the most recent advances – strong but almost invisible foundation wear that was also comfortable to wear and easy to wash and dry.

In 1956, Nancy Mitford wrote that it was U to say 'stays' and non-U to say 'corsets' in her snobbish round-up of OK terminology but really, in the welter of post-war foundation wear, it was often difficult to put a precise definition to any one name:[1] one person's girdle is another's roll-on and many women identify what they wear by a brand name.

Most of the garments mentioned here had suspenders attached, at least until well after the advent of tights in the 1960s, and most were fairly subdued and discreet in colour and fabric although 1957 did see a girdle from Warner on sale with flower-embroidered front panels, decorated with gold thread and a pantie-girdle with colour rhinestones and diamanté stars! The 1970s also brought printed floral patterns as with other lingerie.

Stockings and Tights

The 1950s saw fully-fashioned stockings on sale in silk, nylon and lisle, but it was the market in nylons – whose name soon became synonymous with stockings – that really boomed. Different weights were available, with first 30-denier for everyday wear and 15-denier for special occasions and later a plethora of qualities and colours especially once stockings had, for most people, come to mean tights. By 1990, for instance it was possible to buy stockings or tights in almost any colour and weight from rust or jade non-run rib to 70-denier navy with Lycra to 5-denier sheers as advertised by Pretty Polly that year.

Although most women wore tights, some older people remained loyal to stockings and there was even a burst of fresh interest in stockings from young women who saw them as glamour items to be worn with sexy suspender belts – they were also made with integral 'garters' (stay-up) to hold them up for this market.

Men

In the 1940s, short- or long-sleeved vests and long pants (the old style with button front) were worn against the cold with singlet and trunks for summer wear. They might be in lambswool or a wool mixture, artificial silk or locknit, usually in cream or white. Flannel and knitted wool body belts were also popular as were string vests from about 1948 – these were sports influenced, probably based on the Aertex mesh style. By the 1980s, men wore vests, if at all, only in winter and then generally plain, sleeveless and neckless. These were largely replaced by the T-shirt.

Braces were used to hold up trousers until the 1960s – all elastic with either leather or braided ends. After this a belt was used instead, braces being used only by the older generation and then in the 1980s as a fashion feature especially by city yuppies. Another standard item that was abandoned during this period was the elastic sock suspender. Men either wore ankle socks or relied on an elasticised element in the sock tops to hold them up.

There was considerable diversification in men's lower undergarments from the 1950s to 1990. Jockey pants with strap styling to the crotch arrived from America and Lyle & Scott marketed the Y front with the inverted Y feature at the crotch. These are now called Y front Jockeys. Boxer shorts in loose

HOM boxer shorts, 1992. Brightly patterned boxer shorts have become a classic of men's underwear.

137

HOM all in one bodysuit for men, 1991/2. The recent simplicity of underwear for women has now extended to menswear.

HOM singlet and shorts, 1991/2. The influence of sportswear is evident in this contemporary set of men's underwear *opposite*.

cotton or cotton mix in everything from chic white to cute Xmas reindeer prints came into Britain from the late 1940s onwards and men also wore slips, slip-ons and briefs. Not all men's pants continued to have a fly front. Heavy underwear is a thing of the past except for specialist thermal wear, for example from Damart Thermawear, for winter sports and outdoor wear. Men's fashion designers, such as Armani, Calvin Klein and Paul Smith, have recently moved into the field of designing underwear, with phenomenal success.

Children

By 1990, children wore attractive, functional underwear that washed easily and kept them decent and warm (enough), whether they were 10 months or 10 years old. From pull-on or wrap-around vests in soft cotton to the T-shirts and simple crop tops of the pre-teenagers, their underwear must have been enviable to anyone who had been a mother, or a child, in the 1940s and 1950s when knitted wool vests, liberty bodices (by then seen as burdensome) and heavy knickers (with elastic that broke!) reigned. Even the plastic pants that made mothers' lives easier did not exist until the 1960 and then still in a material less comfortable and flexible than that used in the 1970s and 1980s.

Even little children adopted a form of body stocking – an under-the-crotch-fastening vest top – as well as the ubiquitous Babygro, often worn as underwear. Boys took on the T-shirt as a vest substitute as well as for outerwear, while girls rejected anything at all restrictive and chose to wear undergarments only as and where they saw it necessary – that meant briefs only in summer for most pre-teen girls. Even the Teenform-type light roll-on of the 1960s, designed especially to appeal to young girls and to free them from heavy controlling underwear, by the 1970s and 1980s seemed itself an imposition rather than a freedom. However prettily printed and trimmed it was simply not seen as either necessary or desirable. The younger end of the market in this area was as good as dead.

1940–90: Making, Wearing and the Industry

Vesting and Divesting

Women in this period became adept at getting dressed and undressed on their own, in a hurry and often in confined spaces. The fewer the items of underwear, the better, for active lives which often involved vigorous exercise and regular travel.

A diverse range of underwear came to co-exist, for a host of variable necklines, hem lengths and clothing forms from strapless evening dresses to bottom-hugging jeans, together with thermals for winter sports, sports lines for exercise routines and, last but not least, underwear as outerwear for dancing in clubs. Interchangeability of underwear for comfort and suitability for various activities meant that a woman might change her underwear more than once a day.

Women's reminiscences of wartime undies display an ability to find humour amidst the sacrifices of war. Wartime issue ensured a good supply of underwear to the many women in the armed services. The WAAF had knitted interlock knickers with fleecy linings and they were issued with generous 'brassières made to fit expanded chests – no casualties on the parade ground that way!' Accidents did happen, though, as in the story of the ATS servicewoman who was on parade wearing bias-cut slipper satin French knickers with side buttons (under her uniform!) when the upper button popped off. With enviable aplomb the lady stepped out of her knickers, tucked them out of sight and continued marching.[1] ATS issue knickers were khaki but regulation knickers were clearly not always worn. WRNS issue included three pairs of navy Directoire-style knickers (of

The Slenderella logo from *Drapers Record*, 1957.

rayon locknit for summer and wool for winter). These were nicknamed 'blackouts'. Knitted items such as woolly knickers and stockings required regular mending and even these had to pass inspection!

Making Do

On the home front, 'make do and mend' became a way of life. A yearly ration of 66 clothing coupons in June 1941 was cut by austerity regulations in spring 1942 to only 48. The writer Barbara Pym, then aged 30, confessed that she 'patche[d] her underwear in the evenings'.[2] Long evening slips of the 1930s, which were out of place anyway in austerity Britain, were remodelled into camiknickers, slips and panties or made into nightwear. *Vogue* in 1942 gave patterns for cutting complete dresses of flowered silk or chiffon to make 'camiknicks', or an evening skirt to make a slip. Slips were made into waist petticoats, petticoats into camiknickers; lengths of ribbon were inset to widen slips, two old pairs of knickers were combined to make one good pair, or a new pair made from an old jersey; brassières were made from scraps, and old silk stockings turned into shoulder pads.

The habit of economy died hard and many vests and pants were cast into rag bags and used for cleaning windows and

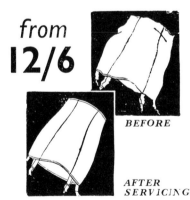
The Corset Renovating Co. advertisement from *Vogue*, August 1942. How to save money and help the war effort.

141

Damart 'Beauty Vest', 1991. Traditionally styled thermal vests remain popular, even fashionable, today.

Triumph sports bra, 1991/2. Sports bras have become standard wear for the multi-activity lifestyle of the 1990s.

dusting well after the war. The extravagance of Christian Dior's full-skirted 'New Look' at first shocked the make-do-and-mend nation but it soon caught on, with women eager to acquire whatever the new styles offered, to replace their worn-out wartime lingerie and corsetry. The styles were distinctively sexy, in a 'don't touch' sort of way. In 1954, Roald Dahl described these new underpinnings: the girdle 'a queer pink undergarment . . . of what appeared to be a strong thick elastic material' with 4-5 inch suspenders 'attached to this elastic armour to grip the tops of the stockings', and second, the brassière, 'a contrivance made of some heavy black material edged with frilly lace . . . another formidable appliance upheld by an arrangement of black straps as skilfully and scientifically rigged as the supporting cables of a suspension bridge.'[3]

Memories of undress from 1960 to 1980 are fresher in the communal memory, encompassing the embarrassment of awkward under-crotch fastenings to teddies, glamourless tights, faulty waist-slip elastic, too-tight briefs under jeans, and a host of nasty synthetic fibres. These stories have yet to be recorded.

Washing and Cleaning

Wartime washing was largely still labour-intensive, and managed with limited resources. By the later 1950s, washing machines were to be found in hotels, schools, and commercial laundries, then in middle-class homes, and in working-class homes in the 1970s and 1980s, together with spin dryers. Washing became easier with the improved machinery. Wool shrinkage problems have largely been solved with special washing programmes on machines ensuring that wool is not matted or scalded. Biological powders have made the whites whiter, replacing the old blue bag. Bleaching has become less necessary and has been positively discouraged for garments containing Lycra. Starch is not needed with polyester and is no longer kept by most households. Electric irons which were in most households by 1950 have been developed with thermostatic controls and steam facilities to remove creases with minimum heat. The hydrophobic properties of nylon and polyester enabled the development of a number of easy-care drip-dry fabrics, which, to apply a quotation from 1950 about the miracle fibre nylon, 'washes "like a rag", dries in next to no time and needs no

ironing . . . looks and feels delightful, and lasts for ever.'[4]

The drawbacks have been that early artificial fabrics were disappointing in performance with the running of dye colours in printed rayons, and prints on polyester as late as the 1970s fading quite quickly. Light-coloured nylons and polyesters can go very muddy-looking if washed in mixed washes, and need a good special wash to retain their original finish. There have been problems with drying Lycra-based garments in direct sunlight, a challenge to the washing-line-in-the-sun tradition. Polyester can burn with a medium iron, and hand washing of fine silk lingerie and fine woollen undies is still practised, for best results, in preference to machine-washing.

Care of Corsets

Corsets in the 1950s could be hand washed in soap suds but not soaked, unlaced or unfastened. The wires from plunge bras could be removed for washing. Towelling dry and slow airing were recommended. Corsets could be returned to companies for laundering (though it was preferred that this was done before sending, as workroom staff threatened strikes in the face of smelly corsets!) and alteration. They were taken in, let out, the bones re-pocketed or replaced, tears mended, and worn panels, elastic, buttons or zips replaced.

Corsets were much loved, much worn, and subtly adapted at home for comfort, with flannelette insertions for warmth over the back, sticking plaster to prevent bones digging in, and sometimes wholesale removal of bones. Squeaky spiral steels were remedied by rubbing on candle wax.

Making, Adopting and Adapting

Fabric shortages in the war led to widespread ingenuity, especially in making underwear, which being out of sight was always the first compromise to economy and hardship. Parachute silk, actually silk, rayon or nylon made up in long triangular segments, was unpicked and re-used for nightdresses, petticoats, brassières and knickers. The nylon was most plentiful, but was reportedly clammy and slippery, and harder to stitch than silk. Much was obtained on the black market, or from machinists working on parachute-making who obtained flawed or half panels, or from army personnel. From 1945, parachutes were on

Spirella factory, November 1957. Erzehbet, from Hungary, was trained as a garment lacer at the Spirella factory in 1957.

open sale in department stores. Jennifer Wayne bought hers that year at Chiesman's in Lewisham: 'This . . . was off coupons . . . always white . . . the bundles were roughly stringed up . . . I had a lot of camiknickers made out of this slithery, paper stuff: in fact my trousseau; if you could call it that, was almost entirely parachute.'[5] The parachute's sections were cut on the cross, so special patterns were issued by, for example, the *Daily Mail*, to ensure careful use of the fabric. It was said that from one-third of a 24-panel parachute you could make two nightdresses, two slips, two pairs camiknickers and four pairs of knickers.

Black-out material could be used to make a nightdress; draughtman's tracing linen was recycled as a brassière or a petticoat, and unrationed dishcloth yarn could be knitted up for vests. Flour sacks were undone and made into children's underwear in Brunswick in Germany, and wadding sewn into underclothing for warmth. At the other extreme, the wartime restrictions on decoration of undergarments were strict: 'One West End milliner found herself in court for the "crime" of embroidering roses and butterflies on camiknickers' during rationing.[6]

Patterns for underwear such as slips, long and short, and bras and French knickers were available in the 1950s, and for slips as foundations to gowns through to the present day. Generally, however, the art of hand- and home-made lingerie has been left to individual designers working with real silk and fine cotton for boutiques, individual enthusiasts making for home consumption, for those requiring 'special sizes', and craftspeople producing garments in polyester crêpe de Chine and polycotton with machine lace insertion, in mock-Edwardian styles.

Buying and Selling

Rationing in the Second World War, under the Utility scheme, meant coupons: four coupons for a petticoat or a slip, for combinations, camiknickers or a corselette; corsets, brassières and belts required three coupons; maternity bras needed only one coupon and a maternity belt no coupons at all. Two vests or two pairs of knickers took six coupons. For men, pants and vests took four coupons (for boys, two); shirts and combinations took eight coupons if they were of wool, five if in any other material.

Corsetry companies survived in the early 1940s by advertising

Lyle & Scott advertisement, 1950s. Superman turns model in this American advertisement for Y fronts and singlets.

Woollaton advertisement from *Drapers Record*, 1956. The inspiration behind this advertisement is evident.

145

Your
Customers
should
wear

AERTEX
UNDERWEAR
& CORSETRY
under
AERTEX

The Cellular Clothing Co. Ltd.
465 Oxford Street, W.1

Aertex advertisement from *Drapers Record*, 1956. A Marilyn Monroe look-alike demonstrates how influential cinema was in the advertising of the 1950s.

Marilyn Monroe in *The Seven Year Itch*, 1955. The archetypal picture of Marilyn Monroe, revealing her panties.

their goods while making diverse items for the war effort, keeping both machinery and staff in work. The Spirella company was under contract to make parachute canopies from 1939 until the end of the war. Gossard made hundreds of experimental kites, thousands of convoy ballons, tens of thousands of lifebelts, sails, distress flags, man-dropper parachute repairs, dinghies, and a total of 639,306 parachutes. The Symington factories made over one million parachutes, plus sand-fly curtains and service apparel including brassières. Other corsetry factories made jungle tents and tarpaulins.

Gossard made 117,688 bras for the Women's Royal Naval Service. Berlei was the only company allowed to put its brand name on the garments it made for the forces. Berlei, Gossard and Silhouette also made ranges of Utility brassières and girdles. Advertising of underwear and corsetry reminded customers of the name even though the goods were in short supply or even non-existent. Berlei ran a successful series of undercover secret service advertisements, with the joint slogans 'Berlei on Active Service', and 'fit your Berlei before your frock', the corseted figure silhouetted against the dressed figure, which set a trend in corsetry advertising for years to come.

In the early post-war period, fine cotton was still difficult to get but 'broderie anglaise' even in nylon sounded alluring to a finery-starved nation. Advertisements in shop catalogues, mail-order catalogues, trade magazines, women's magazines, and company literature lauded the qualities of the new man-made fibres, and described in minute detail each successive new fibre and brand name. Advertising became more risqué as censorship eased up. Advertisements appeared in newspapers and then on television with such companies as American Playtex advertising its 'Cross-your-heart bra' and 'Living girdle', and Silhouette promoting the 'Little X'.

The industry became more formalized during and just after the war. In 1943, the Corset Guild of Great Britain was founded. National Corset Week started in Britain in 1952. In 1955, the Corset and Brassière Council was formed in America. Regular international fairs of lingerie and corsetry have taken place since the 1960s, and company and trade magazines have fostered the perpetuation of this specialized industry.

Slogans flourished to promote the idea that bras and girdles were integral to a woman's sense of herself and to encapsulate ideas of feminine beauty blossoming from beneath, with lines like 'English Rose the flower of modern foundations', 'Next to myself I like Vedonis' and 'Triumph has the bra for the way you are'. In the 1950s it was fashionable to use French names to advertise, hence 'Très Secrète' for an inflatable bra, which the French conversely called '*le soutien-gorge* Very Secret'. Silhouette brought out the 'Little X' stretch corset in 1956 and advertised it using a girl in a black leotard wearing a white bra and girdle, quite a revolutionary method of display at the time, leading to dark models being used for light clothes and vice versa.

In 1957, the trim-line 'Living girdle' by Playtex was sold in a slim tube, and with the new self-service merchandising, from 1958, manufacturers realised that packaging had to be attractive to sell the goods. The habit of giving names instead of numbers to corsetry in the early 1960s was also intended to widen its appeal, one of the foremost instances being Berlei's 'Gay Slant' range of 1962.

One of the latest and most extraordinarily successful lines of advertising has been of men's underwear on women. In September 1982, Calvin Klein advertised his men's underwear in this way 'because of his hunch that girls in boys' pants look completely different from boys.'[7] The result grabbed headlines, changed the women's underwear industry around to offering sporty styles, as well as turning over more than $70 million in its first year.

In fact the world of underwear has changed enormously over the years from 1940 to 1990 in spite of certain popular lines such as the Gossard WonderBra and Playtex's Cross-your-Heart bra and Triumph's Doreen selling on and on. There is still a market for goods produced on machines 50 years old but whereas bra-making is a new industry of this century and flourishes, traditional corsetry only just survives and several major companies closed down in the 1980s. One of these was Spirella, which in the late 1950s and early 1960s had been doing very well with profits in 1964 at their highest ever. At its peak, Spirella employed 2,000 people and sold 200,000 corsets a year; it had 6,000 'consultants' (fitters). Spencers, another market leader, once had 2,000 fitters and 600 office/factory staff but by 1986 was down to 250 fitters and 200 staff and has now closed down completely.

Scandale advertisement, *c*1940s
Imaginative advertising by the French company Scandale, for its pantie-girdle and bra.

'Lillyets' by Triumph, 1992. Relaxed undressing with this front-lacing bra in circular knit blue jean – look fabric with white stretch lace.

This period also saw a number of smaller corsetry companies, often founded by women, being taken over by big names, for instance Courtaulds took over Gossard in 1959, Symingtons in 1967 and Berlei in about 1984. In 1955, Berlei had its own journal, *Fitting News* with regional and personnel news, information and hints, such as how to sterilize fitters' tapes; it employed thousands of trained corsetières and had been running training courses since 1932. In the late 1980s, Triumph (who make for Marks & Spencer as well as under their own name) acquired HOM, the French manufacturer of quality menswear.

And if underwear was a £2 billion a year industry in Britain in the late 1980s then Marks & Spencer surely deserve a mention as the mainstay of this market. Dubbed by the *Telegraph* in 1988 'the guardians of the nation's nether regions', Marks & Spencer alone accounted in 1983 for one-third of underwear sales, and by April 1988 sold 19,000 pairs of knickers daily from their flagship Marble Arch store in London alone.

Other success stories of the 1980s in the UK have been the niche operators, setting up in subways, airports, and shopping centres as well as the high street, for instance Knickerbox set up by Janie Godber and Stephen Schaffer, who, by 1990, had 35 shops and over 150 staff.

Technological Innovation

Most of the big companies have been involved in the technological advances of these years. Berlei, for example began to use Spandex fibres such as Lycra in its bras in 1962 after exhaustive testing of its properties, which include being unaffected by perspiration and body oils (or deodorants), resistant to abrasion and distortion, and remaining soft and supple. It can safely be machine washed and dried – though it should not be boiled, bleached or ironed (no fabric is perfect!).

Some innovations are in fabric cut rather than content. In 1964, Berlei's 'Unda lift' model was the first press-cut bra in Britain. With this method the press cutter uses metal dies to cut through all the layers of material, though some garments still have to be cut using a band knife which requires a skilled cutter.

There is also new machinery which is able to work at up to 5,000 stitches a minute and can cope easily with working with the new elastics. One unique machine, designed and built by engineers at Triumph, forms the cups for seam-free bras - in the technique known as moulding which they pioneered (as they did also the heat-sealed bra strap in 1980). The mouldings of thermoplastic fibres into undergarments is in fact one of the really big improvements of recent decades, enabling sheer, see-through fabrics to provide support and control as required – so, goodbye to bulk. Nylon, cotton polyester, Lycra tricot and knitted Simplex were among fabrics being used for moulded undergarments in the 1970s and 1980s and it is expected that this area will see continued developments in the future.

Now that bras are apparently the future in underwear, this is the field in which there is the fiercest competition – so much so that computers have been brought in to speed up their design and manufacture. This is known as CADCAM, computer-aided design and computer-aided manufacturing.

Back to the Future

There is no denying that the latter half of the twentieth century has seen a revolution in the range of materials available for the construction of underwear. Elastic fabrics, and Lycra in particular, have allowed for a new simplicity in the design and manufacture of undergarments which are both flattering and practical. These materials, although initially developed for underwear, have in turn had a great impact on the design of outerwear. Leggings and cropped bra-tops, along with all manner of cotton/Lycra-mix clothing, are the preferred everyday wear of the vast majority of younger women.

The radical simplicity of new designs in underwear, seen first in the Utility clothing of the 1940s and facilitated later by the availability of new materials, has more in common with the earliest forms of undergarments than with the figure-contorting fantasies of intervening centuries.

Most of all, new materials have made the construction of basic support so simple that the two design considerations of form and function are no longer so inflexibly associated. Women may enjoy the look of times gone by, through details which recall Edwardian or 1920s underwear, without the painful structures formerly employed. Freedom and variety have replaced the voluntary tortures undergone by women who previously endured elaborate contraptions designed to make ideal shapes out of ordinary bodies.

Novelty 'Mozart bra' by Triumph, 1991. When the bra is fastened, a speaker concealed under the arm plays the tune 'twinkle twinkle little star', (Mozart 1778 – a French nursery tune); whilst tiny lights on the cups blink on and off like stars.

Appendices

Notes

Introduction
1 Barbara Pym 1934 in *A Very Private Eye – The Diaries, Letters and Notebooks of Barbara Pym* edited by Hazel Holt and Hilary Pym (London 1985)
2 *Quant by Quant* Mary Quant (London 1966)

Chapter 1
1 Cretan snake goddess c2000 BC (Mansell Collection)
2 Villa Armerina, Sicily, C4th AD (both this and the above are illustrated in *Dress and Undress: A History of Women's Underwear* by Elizabeth Ewing (Batsford, London 1978), and *From Whalebone to See-Through: A History of Body Packaging* by Michael Colmer) (Cassell Australia Ltd. 1979)
3 'New Year's Gifts to Queen Mary in 1556', printed in *Illustrations of the Manners and Expenses of... the 15th, 16th and 17th Centuries* edited by John Nichols (London 1797)
4 *The Malcontent* John Marston (c1603) IV ii 48
5 'To the Maides to walke abroad' Robert Herrick c1640
6 'Epigrams of Nice Wives' from *The Selected Works of Robert Crowley*
7 September 1580: B.L. Egerton f158 v (quoted in Janet Arnold's *Queen Elizabeth's Wardrobe Unlock'd* (Leeds 1988) p198)
8 *The Merry Wives of Windsor* William Shakespeare III iii 69
9 Venetian Calender Vol XV (quoted in Norah Waugh's *Corsets and Crinolines* (Batsford, 1964) p33)

Chapter 2
1 *The Art of Dress* 1717
2 *Salisbury Journal* 1753
3 *The Letters and Journals of Lady Mary Coke Vol 1 1756–67* edited by J.A. Home (Edinburgh 1889)
4 Horace Walpole *Letters* (quoted Waugh *op. cit.* p 65)
5 Francis Place 1824 *Add.* MS 27827 f52

Chapter 3
1 *The Times* 1799 (quoted in *The History of Underclothes* by C. Willet & Phyllis Cunnington with revisions by A.D. Mansfield & Valerie Mansfield, Faber, 1981, p108)

2 *Muffs and Morals* by Pearl Binder (London, 1953)
3 *La Belle Assemblée* February 1814
4 *Letters of Mrs J.W. Carlyle* (quoted Waugh *op. cit.* p134)
5 *The Times* 1796
6 *Glenbevie Journals* 1811 edited by F. Bickley 1928 (quoted Cunnington *op. cit.* p70)
7 *The Norfolk Chronicle* April 10 1802
8 *La Belle Assemblée* December 1806, stays by Mrs Harman, her Majesty's corset and staymaker
9 *La Belle Assemblée* September 1814
10 *The Plain Speaker* by Hazlitt (quoted Waugh *op. cit.* p133)
11 *Monthly Journal of Fashion* May 1832

Chapter 4
1 Advertised in *Punch* in 1857 Vol 32
2 Dr Jaeger's book *Health Culture*, was published in a new revised edition by Dr Jaeger's Sanitary Woollen System Co. Ltd in 1907, translated by Lewis R.S. Tomalin

Chapter 5
1 *How to Dress on £15 Per Year, As a Lady*, by A Lady (Mrs Millicent W. Cook) (London, 1873)

Chapter 6
1 *Letter to the Ladies of England* August 1 1863
2 *My Memories of Six Reigns* by Princess Marie Louise (Penguin 1959)
3 Quoted in *Vogue* (September 1950)

Chapter 7
1 The 'Gibson Girl' was immortalized in the drawings of American artist Charles Dana Gibson, and had an exaggerated S-shaped figure. She was embodied on the London stage by the actress Camille Clifford

Chapter 8
1 Advertisement for Cappers in the *Ladies Field* of June 14 1902
2 Shirer & Haddon Cheltenham, Annual Winter Sale 1892

Chapter 9
1 *The Edwardians* by Vita Sackville-West, (first published Penguin, 1930)
2 *Portrait of My Victorian Youth* by Alice Pollock c1890, (Johnson, London, 1971)
3 *Rose: My Life in Service* by Rosina Harrison, (Futura, 1976)
4 *Giggling in the Shrubbery* by Arthur Marshall, (Fontana, 1986)

Chapter 10
1 *Baby Doll, A Face in the Crowd* directed by Elia Kazan in 1956

Chapter 11
1 *Noblesse Oblige* by Nancy Mitford (1956)

Chapter 12
1 *Betty Snow in Women in Airforce Blue* by Beryl E. Escott (Wellinborough, 1989)
2 Barbara Pym (*op. cit*)
3 *Someone Like You* by Roald Dahl, (London 1954)
4 Advertisement in *Woman's Journal*, (August 1 1950)
5 *The Purple Dress* by Jennifer Wayne, (Gollancz 1979)
6 *You'll Never be 16 Again* by Peter Everett (BBC Publications 1986)
7 Article in *Airport* (March 1989) Calvin Klein by Marion Hume

Glossary

Underwear: Female unless otherwise stated.
abbr. = abbreviation, dim. = diminutive French terms have often been used in fashion magazines and may indicate origins of garments and terminology in some instances. Bracketed dates indicate first popular usage of the term in this context. Sources are indicated where possible. Where terms changed their meaning during the periods covered by this book this is indicated. It will be noticed that anything with the suffix '-ette' seems to be derivative of and/or smaller than another core garment. Key terms for combination garments are given, but many others were invented and may be deduced from the guidelines indicated here.

Undergarments

BALAYEUSE (by 1880s): A removable ruffle attached to the inside hem of a skirt or *underskirt(q.v.)* to protect the dress from collecting dirt.
BANDEAU (by 1921 Gossard catalogue): Form of *brassière(q.v.)* which hooks at the back. A lightweight garment comprising a narrow strip or strips of fabric with minimal shaping.
BASQUE: Section of bodice below waist, shaped to hips; late C20th name for *corset(q.v.)*.
BELT: In the late C19th a type of *corset(q.v.)* with inner belt or (or horizontal straps) to constrict abdomen, buttocks and upper thighs. Also synonymous with C20th *girdle(q.v.)*. The term was frequently applied to male corsets worn for health, beauty or sport.
BENTS (C16th): Stiffening for *stays(q.v.)*, farthingale or *hoop(q.v.)* made from bunches of hollow-stemmed reeds.

BLOOMERS (1851): Long, baggy, Turkish-style trousers worn by dress reformer Amelia Bloomer. American term for *Directoire knickers(q.v.)* in the 1920s.

BODIES (a pair of) (C16th): Rigid covering for the upper body made in two halves laced together, and worn over the *smock(q.v.)*. The outerwear of the whalebone-stiffened C17th bodice becomes underwear in the C18th when this garment is termed 'a pair of *stays(q.v.)*'.

BODY (1986): Allied to the *bodystocking(q.v.)*. A skin-tight stretch garment sleeved or sleeveless, covering the torso and fastening under the *crotch(q.v.)*. Worn next to the skin, with or without *bra(q.v.)* to give a smooth line. Forerunners include the *pantie-corselette(q.v.)* and bodyshaper (1970s onwards).

BODY BELT: A humble, unisex, tubular knitted garment worn next to the skin to ward off winter chills (persisting into the C20th).

BODYSTOCKING (1960s): Skin-tight stretch garment worn next to the skin, covering the body from neck to ankles and wrists. Principally worn by dancers or athletes but for fashion under tight clothing to simulate nudity.

BOSOM FRIENDS (c1800): Padding or bunched fabric worn primarily to augment the chest, but also as protection from the cold.

BOXER SHORTS (1940s): Male underpants, generally loose-fitting and falling to upper or mid-thigh from an elasticated waistband.

BRA (1937): Abbr. *brassière(q.v.)*: Breast support, developed from simple *bandeau(q.v.)*. Strapped or strapless, for sport, nursing or fashion. Now with separate cups, reinforced by stitching, padding or underwiring.

BRACES (a pair of) (c1820): (USA Suspenders): Over-the-shoulder straps to suspend men's trousers, fastening to waistband by means of buttons and later metal clasps.

BRA SIZES (1935): A system of sizing introduced by Warner Bros. based on the difference between the circumference below the bust and at its widest point. Four cup sizes were introduced (A, B, C, D) and later sizes from AAA increasing to G became available to allow for a full bust on an otherwise slim figure and vice versa.

BRA SLIP (c1932 Maidenform 'costume slip'): *Petticoat(q.v.)* with brassière-shaped top giving bust support. Originated in America with built-in lastex brassière, revived and promoted by Berlei in 1969 as the 'new mini bra-slip'.

BRASSETTE (c1925): A form of *corse-*

lette(q.v.). Veco registered *brassière(q.v.)* and *corset(q.v.)* combined.

BRASSIÈRE (1907 (USA), 1912 *The Lady*): A garment shaped solely to bind or later support and uplift the bust, superseding the *bust bodice(q.v.)*. Either shaped like a *bandeau(q.v.)* or with a triangular piece covering and supporting each breast.

BRETELLES (c1870s): French term for *braces(q.v.)*. Two bands worn over shoulder, attached to waistband front and back to suspend a skirt. Also a term for decorative over-the-shoulder trimming.

BRIEFS (a pair of) (1950s): Close-fitting, legless *panties(q.v.)*, diminishing in depth and cut high on the leg or hip into the 1990s.

BUSK (C16th): Piece of wood, whalebone, horn, ivory or steel slotted into front of *stays(q.v.)* to hold the torso erect. The integral front section of C19th *corset(q.v.)* shaped to control the abdomen, and also its steel stud and eye fastening.

BUST BODICE (c1890): Covering for bust before the advent of the *brassière(q.v.)* Usually with straps and sometimes lightly boned at sides and/or front for 'mono-bosom' effect.

BUSTIER (c1947): A *long-line brassière(q.v.)*, often strapless. *Punch* 16th March 1955 defined this garment as 'a deep and waisted brassière which embraces rib and hip-bones'.

BUST IMPROVER (1840s): Padding sewn in or inserted into pockets in the dress or *corset(q.v.)* to augment the bosom. In the late C19th several devices were patented to mimic breasts, made of rubber or braided wire.

BUSTLE (by 1839): An artificial structure giving extension or fullness to skirts at the back; formed of fabric pads, frills of horsehair-stiffened cloth, or frames of wire. Most conspicuous throughout the 1870s-80s when it was more popularly known by the French term *tournure(q.v.)*.

B.V.D.s (1890s) (USA): Male *combinations(q.v.)* or *union suit(q.v.)* which became synonymous with the name of its manufacturers Bradley, Voorhies and Day (established USA 1876).

CAMI-BOCKERS (c1926): *Camisole (q.v.)* and *Directoire knickers(q.v.)* combined. Generally with thin straps and of lightweight fabric.

CAMIKNICKERS (c1916): *Camisole(q.v.)* or *chemise(q.v.)* and *French knickers(q.v.)* combined; popular 1920s-30s and revived 1980s. One stepped into them, slid the straps over the shoulders and fastened the buttons below the *crotch(q.v.)*.

CAMISOLE (c1840s): Derived from the

French word for a bed-jacket or loose corset tied in front with ribbons. The word was applied to an underbodice or *corset-cover(q.v.)* (Fr. *cache-corset*) from c1840. Generally decorated, made of linen or cotton until c1900, later knitted or crocheted. By c1915 it could be worn over the *bust bodice(q.v.)* or *brassière(q.v.)*, trimmed to supplement the bust, or discarded as preferred.

CHEMILETTE (1880s): A combination garment made of linen or cotton advocated by UK and USA dress reformers. Combining *chemise(q.v.)* and *drawers(q.v.)* it could be worn over the woollen *combinations(q.v.)* or *union suit(q.v.)*.

CHEMISE (c1790): New term for the female smock or shift, the sleeveless knee-length linen, cotton or silk garment worn next to the skin. By 1925 it gave way to a shorter garment, the 'chemise-vest', and then to the shorter *vest(q.v.)*. By 1823 the Envelope chemise was invented which fastened between the legs with a strap or gusset.

CHEMISETTE (c1830): Dim. *chemise(q.v.)*: Like the *habit-shirt(q.v.)* a vestigial garment designed to show at the neck. A false chemise-front, or modesty-piece popular throughout the C19th diminishing almost to a collar during the 1880s.

COMBINATIONS (c1874): Dress reformers advocated this garment for its warmth and reduced bulk. The female version combined the *chemise(q.v.)* and *drawers(q.v.)*, to create the fashionable slim line. It was available in both winter and summer versions, in wool or cotton. Both short and long-sleeved/legged versions remained popular to 1930.

CORSELETTE (c1921): Occasionally a term for a diminutive waist-encircling *corset(q.v.)* (corselet 1893), but generally the term for a garment combining the functions of a *brassière(q.v.)* and *girdle(q.v.)*. Therefore a tubular garment, giving a smooth line, often with shoulder straps and stocking suspenders attached.

CORSET (1789 *Lady's Monthly Museum*): The new term for the C18th *stays(q.v.)* or C16th pair of *bodies(q.v.)*. The stiffened garment which supported and shaped the torso. Principally a female fashion garment but occasionally worn for male fashion, and by both sexes for medical reasons to correct posture. Generally back-lacing and front-fastening.

CORSET-COVER (c1840): The cotton underbodies which provided the easily laundered buffering layer between dress and corset. Less prosaically termed a *camisole(q.v.)*.

CORSET WAIST: American term for early *brassière(q.v.)*, and also for a type of snug-fitting *liberty bodice(q.v.)* worn by children.

CRINOLETTE (1870s): Half crinoline; A cage *crinoline(q.v.)* with hoops only at the back.

CRINOLINE: Term derived from the French *crin* for horsehair which was originally used to stiffen the *lin* (linen) of the *petticoat(q.v.)*. From the mid-1850s a cage-like structure of spring steels in hoops of increasing diameter held together with curved steel ribs or tapes, sometimes covered in part with fabric. Term subsequently applied to the full skirts of the 1950s.

CROPPED TOP (1980s): A stretch *bra(q.v.)* in the form of a short and tight-fitting *vest(q.v.)*, sometimes with elastic under the bust and built-up shoulders.

CROTCH: Rectangular or diamond-shaped *gusset(q.v.)* between the legs of *pants(q.v.)* or *knickers(q.v.)*.

CUIRASS (c1870): Form of bodice that was boned and lined to fit closely to the upper body and hips, therefore resembling an external *corset(q.v.)*. Term derived from upper body armour which it resembled.

CUTIES (1950s): False breasts.

DENIER: A unit of weight originally denoting the fineness of silk, now also used to define the fibre filament of synthetic fabrics. Applied to hosiery, as a gauge of the opacity of the fabric. The lower the denier the thinner the filament, therefore the sheerer the *tights(q.v.)* or *stockings(q.v.)*.

DICKEY: C18th term for an underpetticoat: By 1811 a sham shirt, a bib-like detachable shirt front.

DIRECTOIRE KNICKERS (c1909): Loose-fitting upper leg coverings, gathered at waist and knee, and held in place with buttons or elastic. Named after the slim-line Directoire period in France and revived to enhance the lean, flowing lines of Paul Poiret's designs.

DRAWERS: Not general female wear until the 1840s. Generally two tubes of fabric gathered onto a waistband, and left open at the crotch, from which closed leg *knickers(q.v.)* developed. Fastened round the waist by means of a drawstring, buttons, or both.

DRESS IMPROVER (c1849): Frame to form *bustle(q.v.)*.

DRESS PRESERVERS/PROTECTORS/ SHIELDS (1840s): Small crescent-shaped chamois pads sewn in to the dress bodice or worn at the armpits to shield the dress fabric from the odour and discolouration of perspiration. They could be attached at the upper arm by means of frilled elastic bracelets.

FALSIES (1950s): False bust, often formed by removable bust pads.

FOUNDATION: Post WW1 *corselette(q.v.)* from America. Popular in 1940s and said to be as comfortable as a second skin.

FRENCH KNICKERS: Short, full *knickers(q.v.)* elasticated or shaped to the waist. Generally of a silky fabric and popular in the 1930s and 1940s.

G-STRING: Minimal *briefs(q.v.)* comprising a thin horizontal waistband joined to fabric triangular at front diminishing to a vertical strip between the buttocks. In the late C20th generally worn by strippers or under tight clothing.

GARTER: Ribbon or band worn around the leg to keep the stocking up before the advent of the *suspender belt(q.v.)* (hence American term 'garter belt').

GESTATION STAYS (C19th): A maternity *corset(q.v.)* with adjustable hip gores, side-lacing, and breast openings, to be worn during pregnancy and in order to restore the figure after the event.

GIRDLE (by 1923 *Harpers Bazaar*): Lightweight *corset(q.v.)* extending from waist to upper thigh, often elasticated or rubberized and fastened with side zips.

GODET, GORE, GUSSET: Triangular pieces of material inserted to shape or strengthen garments, or give ease of movement. Generally more economical than cutting fabric to shape, and less bulky than gathering.

HABIT SHIRT (c1800): A kind of *chemisette(q.v.)* generally of cotton with upstanding collar or ruff worn to show under outer bodice.

HALF SLIP (c1950): A *petticoat(q.v.)* reaching from waist to knee, generally worn to reduce static between *nylons(q.v.)* and skirt rather than providing bulk like a waist *petticoat(q.v.)*

HIP-SPRING: Hip measurement minus waist measurement usually calculated at 9″ – 13″.

HOOK SIDE: Side-fastening *girdle(q.v.)* or *corset(q.v.)*

HOOP (C18th): Oval-shaped understructure to extend the hips, usually of linen with cane or whalebone. Reached its apex in C18th fashion in the 1740s but retained for English Court wear until 1820.

HOSE: Popular term for close-fitting foot and leg covering from C12th-C19th. Revived 1921 for *stockings(q.v.)* or knee-length socks (*The Lady*).

INEXPRESSIBLES (c1805): Men's tight-fitting outer leg coverings, or trousers, becoming a prudish euphemism for drawers in the mid-C19th.

JOCK-STRAP: The male equivalent of the *G-string(q.v.)*. A pouch suspended from the waist by an elasticated band, worn by male athletes or dancers to support and protect their genitalia.

JOCKEYS: Short, close-fitting underdrawers worn by men.

JUMPS: C18th underbodice, a looser alternative to the rigid *stays(q.v.)*. Generally front-fastening, and worn for informal undress or indisposition.

KNICKERBOCKERS (a pair of) (by 1872 *Young Englishwoman*): Voluminous *drawers(q.v.)* gathered at waist and knee. Named for their resemblance to the breeches worn by Washington Irving's fictional C17th Dutch family of that name.

KNICKERS (1822 *The Queen*): Abbr. knickerbockers: The term for *drawers(q.v.)* which were closed under the *crotch(q.v.)*. Popular term even for open drawers (q.v.) from 1890 onwards.

LIBERTY BODICE: Close-fitting underbodice for children manufactured by Symingtons from 1908-1970s. Similar 'stay bands' (UK) or 'corset waists' (USA) had been manufactured by other firms since 1880s and continued to be made into 1980s. A reminder of posture-forming stiffened *stays(q.v.)* it was worn principally for warmth and had buttons at the waist to anchor the remaining nethergarments snugly to it.

LINGERIE: French word for linen draper; used for selected items of nightwear and underlinen from the 1830s, coming to mean fine luxury underwear in silk and lace in the 1890s.

LONG-LINE BRASSIÈRE (c1950s): Bust support extending down to waist, for heavier figures. Similar to *bustier(q.v.)* but with shoulder straps. Also called a 'deep brassière'.

LONG JOHNS (c1890): Type of *union suit(q.v.)* named after John L. Sullivan. Generally a masculine garment worn for warmth, consisting of waist to ankle-length woollen underpants.

MERRY WIDOW (1951): A corset made by Warner's and named after Lehar's operetta. Creating an hour-glass shape it had half-cup bust support and long stocking suspenders.

NYLONS 1940s): Popular term for nylon stockings from the 1940s-60s.

PANNIER: French term for the C18th side hoops, revived for the bunched hip drapery, or *bustle(q.v.)* of the late 1860s-80s.

PANTALETTES: C19th term derived from the male outer leg covering the 'Pantaloon'. Frilled, ankle-length *loose drawers(q.v.)* worn by young girls to c1825 and then also gradually adopted by their mothers.

PANTIE (c1905): (dim. pantaloons): Generally legless and briefer cut than *knickers(q.v.)*, popular term from the 1930s.

PANTIE CORSELETTE (c1960): Full body *corselette(q.v.)* with under-crotch fastening of *pantie(q.v.)*.

PANTIE GIRDLE (c1941): Lightly elasticated waist *girdle(q.v.)* with crotch piece or *pantie(q.v.)* to separate thighs, and to prevent it riding up.

PANTS (a pair of): Abbr. pantaloons: Term for male *drawers(q.v.)* since the C19th, now also applied to female *knickers(q.v.)* whilst the male garment is generally styled 'underpants'. Close-fitting, long or short, but steadily decreasing in length from the 1920s-80s to become *briefs(q.v.)*.

PASSION KILLERS (1940s): Women's *pants(q.v.)*, especially thick and voluminous wartime service *knickers(q.v.)* elasticated at waist and upper thighs.

PETTICOAT: C15th outergarment to C19th undergarment, waist to ankle-length skirt to *underskirt(q.v.)*. By the C20th the full-length *princess slip(q.v.)* was also called a petticoat.

PETTICOAT BODICE: Underbodice, *corset-cover(q.v.)* or *camisole(q.v.)*, worn with waist *petticoat(q.v.)*, or attached to it.

PETTI-KNICKERS (1947): *Knickers(q.v.)* and waist *petticoat(q.v.)* combined.

PLUMET PETTICOAT: Trained *petticoat(q.v.)* for wearing under the trained skirt of the late 1870s.

PRINCESS PETTICOAT (c1876): A combined undergarment, also later called a 'bodyskirt', performing the function of the *camisole(q.v.)* and waist *petticoat(q.v.)* but cut in gored panels without a waist seam for reduced bulk. It was designed for wearing under the close-fitting Princess-line dresses (named after Alexandra Princess of Wales).

RIBBON CORSET (c1904): A lightweight *corset(q.v.)* worn for sport or relaxation. Formed of horizontal elastic strips mounted on a shaped side seam, it encircled the waist and top of the hips, to give abdominal support.

ROLL-ON (c1932): Unboned, elasticated *girdle(q.v.)*, tubular and without fastenings, hence the name.

SANITARY BELT ('Ladies Belt' 1849): Two strips of fabric one encircling the waist, the other looping between the legs to hold a sanitary towel or dressing in place.

SHIFT: Loose unstructured linen garment worn next to the skin, made of oblong lengths of cloth, or shaped with side gores. Synonymous with the terms *smock(q.v.)* and *chemise(q.v.)*.

SINGLET: An unlined male garment (as opposed to the lined 'doublet'), worn next to the skin for warmth. In the C20th the term has come to denote a scoop-necked, sleeveless and scantily-cut *vest(q.v.)*.

SLEEVE SUPPORTS: Crescent-shaped pads of linen or cotton stuffed with down, used to bulk out voluminous sleeves, or sleeve heads (e.g. 1830s).

SLIP: Early C19th coloured undergown designed to show through diaphanous outer garment. Term translated to C20th sleeveless underpetticoat dependent from shoulder or waist (half-slip). Generally used to diminish bulk rather than create it.

SMOCK (C11th): Earlier term for *shift(q.v.)* replaced by the term *chemise(q.v.)* in the 1830s.

SPENCER: A warm underbodice of knitted wool worn throughout the C19th and persisting through the C20th.

STAYS: (a pair of): C17th & C18th term for the boned underbodice previously known as a 'pair of *bodies(q.v.)*'. The term persisted into the C19th but was more usually replaced by its French equivalent the *corset(q.v.)*. The term was also applied to the stiff inserts of whalebone or steel which shaped this garment.

STEP-IN (1930s): Type of *girdle(q.v.)* without fastenings made with vertical boning and elasticated panels. The semi step-in had fastening extending only part of the way down.

STOCKINGS (C16th): Woven or knitted coverings for the feet and legs, equivalent to *hose(q.v.)*.

STRING VEST (c1948): Minimal male sleeveless *singlet(q.v.)* of large mesh knit introduced for use by US servicemen in the tropics.

SUSPENDER BELT (c1876) (USA garter belt): Progressed from over-the-shoulder harness to waistband with suspended attachments for holding up *stockings(q.v.)*, first with buttons, then with metal loops. Integral suspenders began to appear attached to the *corset(q.v.)* from c1900 and were later attached to back and front of *girdle(q.v.)* or *corselette(q.v.)* as an alternative to the separate suspender belt, which persists till the present.

TANGA (1980s): Brief *pants(q.v.)* made up of two triangles of fabric joined at the hips by thin strips.

TANGO CORSET (c1914): Short lightweight *corset(q.v.)* for dancing in, forerunner of the *girdle(q.v.)*.

TANGO KNICKERS (c1913): Voluminous *knickers(q.v.)* designed for maximum leg-movement. Formed from an oblong of lightweight fabric looped back on itself to the waistband and partially stitched down each side to form leg openings.

TEDDY (c1924): A combination garment of US origin combining *camisole(q.v.)* and *knickers(q.v.)*, generally boneless and loose-fitting. Revived in the 1960s-90s as an updated term for *camiknickers(q.v.)*.

TIGHTS (1965) (USA Panti-hose): A one-piece stretch garment covering the feet and legs up to the waist, combining the functions of *stockings(q.v.)* and *pants(q.v.)*. In theatrical use since the C19th.

TOURNURE: French word for *bustle(q.v.)* pad or structure used to extend the skirt at back or sides, in popular use c1868-80s.

TROUSERS: Term for girl's and boy's *pantalettes(q.v.)* or *drawers(q.v.)* from c1820-60s.

TRUNKS (1930s): Underpants worn by men and boys. Generally loose-legged and ending above the knee.

UNDERSKIRT: The main starched or decorated *petticoat(q.v.)* or that worn immediately below the main garment which may be coloured and designed to show through the outer layer.

UNION SUIT (1880s) (USA): American equivalent of *combinations(q.v.)* advocated by dress reformers, made of knitted wool or silk. The male garment was termed *B.V.D.s(q.v.)*.

VEST: C17th under-waistcoat for men (sleeved or sleeveless) developing by the C19th into a T-shaped or camisole-like garment for men and women, worn for warmth. By the C20th it was often knitted without fastenings and worn next to the skin or over the *bra(q.v.)*; the usual adjunct to *knickers(q.v.)* since the 1930s for men, women and children alike).

WASPIE: Term applied to the belt-like corsets of the late 1940s and 1950s designed to create a small waist.

WASP WAIST: Small waist created by tight-lacing. Term used by Mrs Delaney in 1775, reappearing in the late 1820s and the 1890s, as well as the 1950s.

Fabrics

ACETATE: Manmade textile fibre made from regenerated cellulose.

AERTEX: Brand name for cotton cellular cloth registered by the Cellular Clothing Co. in 1896.

ALPACA: Lustrous fabric of Alpaca goat's wool (and sometimes silk). First created by Sir Titus Salt in 1838.

ANTRON: Du Pont brand name for a type of *nylon(q.v.)*.

ARTIFICIAL DYES: Dyes from a chemical base. The first of the many aniline dyes was a mauve developed in 1856 by William Perkins.

ARTIFICIAL SILK: The first manmade textile fibre manufactured in France in 1885. Named 'Chardonnet' after its inventor, or 'art silk'.

BALEINE: Whalebone from the Baleine whale.

BATISTE: Fine, sheer, plain weave linen (later cotton or polyester).

BRI-NYLON: Brand name for *nylon(q.v.)* manufactured by I.C.I. Fibres Ltd.

BROCADE: Textile woven with raised pattern, (originally of gold or silver), resembling embroidery.

BROCATELLE: Imitation *brocade(q.v.)*, usually of silk or wool (normally has a satin or twill figure on a plain or satin ground).

BROCHÉ: Silk, cotton or *rayon(q.v.)* fabric with satin surface pattern woven on Jacquard loom – loosely, the corsetry term for *brocade(q.v.)*.

BRODERIE ANGLAISE: Hand or machine worked whitework embroidery on cotton, muslin or silk. Also known as Madeira work or eyelet embroidery.

CALICO: Hardwearing plain weave cotton cloth.

CAMBRIC: Fine white linen, originally from Cambrai, now a cotton cloth – firmer and heavier than *nainsook(q.v.)*.

CANE: Hollow stems of giant reeds – strong and flexible.

CASHMERE: Fine, soft and warm wool from the Kashmir goat.

CELANESE: Tradename registered in 1921 for *artificial silk(q.v.)* (viscose rayon) produced by British Celanese Ltd.

CELON: By 1964 Courtaulds UK brand name for *nylon(q.v.)*.

CHIFFONELLE: A diaphanous plain weave fabric of silk or *nylon(q.v.)*.

CHLOROFIBRE: Used for thermal underwear.

CORD: Twisted threads stitched between layers of material for stiffening, or narrow rouleaux padded with cotton wool.

COUTIL: Firm twilled cotton, or cotton and *rayon(q.v.)* fabric, closely woven in herringbone construction.

DRILL: Firm and strong twilled linen or cotton fabric.

ELASTIC: Threads of *rubber(q.v.)* encased in silk or cotton.

FLANNEL: Twill or plain weave napped woollen stuff, of varying fineness.

FLANNELETTE: Cotton imitation of *flannel(q.v.)*.

HELANCA: Tradename for stretch nylon yarn made by Heberlein & Co., Switzerland.

HORROCKSES: Form of *longcloth(q.v.)* named after its late C19th manufacturer.

HORSEHAIR: (*Fr. Crin*): Used to stiffen fabric in the C18th and C19th.

JACQUARD: Figured fabric from a Jacquard loom.

JAP SHAN: Tradename for *viyella(q.v.)* made by William Hollins and Co.

JAP SILK: Paper silk from Northern China.

LASTEX: 1931 Tradename of the US Rubber Co. for their strips of *rubber(q.v.)* covered with silk, cotton, wool or rayon to form a yarn.

LASTING: A durable cloth of twisted yarn.

LATEX: Sticky sap from the Para rubber tree which is treated to form the raw material for *rubber(q.v.)*.

LAWN: Fine, plain weave linen or cotton, sheerer than *nainsook(q.v.)*.

LEAVERS LACE: Machine-made lace, named after its inventor John Leavers.

LENO: A mesh-like cotton gauze, formed by twisting the warp yarns before weaving.

LISLE: Two-ply mercerised cotton yarn usually knitted for stockings. Originally from Lille, France.

LONGCLOTH: Strong plain weave cotton.

LYCRA: Synthetic elastomeric fibre, with good recovery properties. Invented by Du Pont USA 1959, and launched in Britain 1960.

MADAPOLLAM: Indian cotton fabric.

MARQUISETTE: Leno weave gauze of cotton, silk, *rayon(q.v.)* or synthetic fibre.

MERINO: Very soft, fine, wool (later mixed with cotton).

MOUSSELINE DE SOIE: (Eng. Silk muslin): A thin, crisp silk organdie, or chiffon.

NAINSOOK: Soft, fine, Indian cotton fabric, with a plain weave. Often mercerised. Slightly coarser than *batiste(q.v.)* and *lawn(q.v.)*.

NINON: Smooth, transparent closely-woven voile of cotton, *rayon(q.v.)*, silk or *nylon(q.v.)*.

NYLON: The first synthetic fibre, a polyamide developed by the Du Pont laboratory in 1938, knitted or woven for stockings and lingerie, and manufactured under a variety of tradenames.

ORLON: A Du Pont tradename for a soft, warm, acrylic used for textiles and knitwear.

POLYESTER: A synthetic fibre, with good washing properties, first developed in 1941 at the laboratory of the Calico Printers Association, Lancashire.

RAYON: The term for *artificial silk(q.v.)* (USA 1924, UK 1929). A manmade fibre made of regenerated cellulose using chemical wood pulp. Developed commercially by Courtaulds from 1905. Knitted rayon is termed locknit.

RUBBER: (abbr. India Rubber): An elastic fibre derived from hardened and (since 1840s) vulcanized *latex(q.v.)* extruded or cut into strips). Now more commonly applied to the synthetic fibres which share its properties.

SHETLAND: Short, curly and silky wool from the Shetland Island sheep.

SPANDEX: USA term for the group of synthetic elastomeric fibres (e.g. *Lycra(q.v.)*, Vyrene, Spanzelle, Glospan, and Blue C.). Given the EC term elastane in 1976.

SPANZELLE: The version of *Lycra(q.v.)* produced by Courtaulds.

SPIRAL STEELS: Used for stiffening corsetry from 1904.

TORCHON LACE: A coarse, simple, loosely woven bobbin lace.

TAFFETA: Originally a plain-weave glossy silk, now a light, crisp, silk or *union cloth(q.v.)*.

TERYLENE: The name given to the first *polyester(q.v.)* fibre discovered in 1941. I.C.I. took over its production.

UNION CLOTH: A fabric of mixed materials, e.g. of cotton and linen.

VILOFT: A soft, absorbent *viscose(q.v.)* made by Courtaulds.

VISCOSE: A process of manufacturing *rayon(q.v.)* discovered by Cross, Bevan and Beadle in 1892, but used by Courtaulds since 1904. Therefore becoming synonymous with the *rayon(q.v.)* fabric manufactured by Courtaulds.

VIYELLA: The propriety name of a cotton and wool twill made by William Hollins & Co. of Nottingham 1894.

VYRENE: Launched in USA by the US Rubber Co. and in Britain by Lastex Yarn and Lactron Thread Co. Ltd.

WATCHSPRING STEEL: Spring steel covered with hard *rubber(q.v.)*, manufactured by Strouse, Adler and Co. c1880.

WHALEBONE: See *Baleine(q.v.)* from the Bay of Biscay, Greenland and the Arctic.

Bibliography

Books

(Published in London unless otherwise stated)

Adburgham, Alison, *Shops and Shopping 1800-1914* (Allen & Unwin, 1964; paperback edition Barrie & Jenkins, 1989)

Arnold, Janet, *A Handbook of Costume* (Macmillan, 1973)

Arnold, Janet, *Patterns of Fashion I, II and 1560-1620* (Macmillan, 1985)

Arnold, Janet, *Queen Elizabeth's Wardrobe Unlock'd* (Marey, Leeds, 1988)

Birbari, Elizabeth, *Dress in Italian Painting* (John Murray, 1975)

Bradfield, Nancy, *Costume in Detail 1730-1930* (Harrap, 1968)

Buck, Anne, *Victorian Costume and Costume Accessories* (Herbert Jenkins, 1961)

Cassell's Household Guide published in 4 volumes (c1868-70)

CIBA Review no 46 'Crinoline and Bustle' by W. Born (CIBA Ltd. Basle, Switzerland, 1943)

Colmer, Michael, *From Whalebone to See Through: A History of Body Packaging* (Cassell Australia Ltd., 1979)

Crawford, M.D.C. & E.G., *The History of Corsets in Pictures* (Fairchild Publications, New York, 1952)

Crawford, M.D.C. & E.G., *The History of Lingerie in Pictures* (Fairchild Publications, New York, 1952)

Cunnington, C.W. & P., *The History of Underclothes* (Michael Joseph, 1951; rev. edn. Faber, 1991)

Druber und Drunter Wiener Damenmode Von 1900-1914 (Exhibition Catalogue; Hermesville 11.4.87—28.2.88)

Earnshaw, Pat, *Lace in Fashion* (Batsford, 1985; Chapter 7 'Lace on Underwear')

Ewing, Elizabeth, *Fashions in Underwear* (Batsford, 1971) Updated as *Dress and Undress: A History of Women's Underwear* (Batsford, 1978; paperback edn. 1989)

Fabri, G.E., *La Mode, Art, Histoire, Société* (Frazietta, Butazzi, 1981) Translated by Bernard Guyader (Livre de Paris, 1983)

Foster, Vanda & Walkley, Christina, *Crinolines and Crimping Irons: Victorian Clothes: How they were cleaned and cared for* (Peter Owen, 1978)

Bernsheim, Alison, *Victorian and Edwardian Fashion: A Photographic Survey* (Dover, New York, 1981) (Originally published as *Fashion and Reality*, Faber, 1963)

Ginsbury, Madeleine, *Victorian Dress in Photographs* (Batsford, 1982)

Kidwell, Claudia & Steele, Valerie, *Men and Women: Dressing the Part* (Smithsonian Institution Press, Washington D.C., 1989)

La Galleria Del Costume/2 (Palazzo Pitti, Firenze, 1986)

Leoty, Ernest, *Le Corset À Travers Les Ages* (Paris, 1893)

Levitt, Sarah, *Victorians Unbutton'd: Registered Designs for Clothing, their Makers and Wearers, 1839-1900* (Allen & Unwin, 1986)

Libron, F. & Clouzot H., *Le Corset Dans L'Art et Les Moeurs du XIIIe au XXe Siècle* (Paris, 1933)

Martin, Richard, *The Undercover Story* (Exhibition Catalogue, Fashion Institute of Technology, New York, 1982, Kyoto Costume Institute, Japan, 1983)

Masel, Marjorie, *The Boxers Project* (Gibbs Smith Utah, 1988, Introductory Chapter: 'Understatement')

Newton, Stella Mary, *Health, Art and Reason: Dress Reformers of the 19th Century* (John Murray, 1974)

Page, Christopher, *Foundations of Fashion: The Symington Collection of Corsetry from 1856-1979* (Leicestershire Museums, 1981)

Pasold, Eric W., *Ladybird, Ladybird: A Story of Private Enterprise* (Manchester University Press, 1977)

Pearce, Arthur W., *The Future Out of the Past* (The Warner Brothers Co., Bridgeport, Connecticut, 1963/4)

Perrot, Philippe, *Les Dessus et Les Dessous de La Bourgeoisie: Une Histoire du Vêtement au XIXe Siècle* (Librarie Arthème, Fayard, 1981)

Probert, Christina, *Lingerie in Vogue Since 1910* (Thames & Hudson, 1982)

Ribeiro, Aileen, *Dress and Morality* (Batsford, 1986)

Rose, Clare, *Children's Clothes* (Batsford, 1989)

Rudofsky, Bernard, *The Unfashionable Human Body* (Doubleday & Co., New York, 1971; Rupert Hart-Davis, 1972)

Steele, Valerie, *Fashion and Eroticism: Ideals of Feminine Beauty from the Victorian Era to the Jazz Age* (Oxford University Press, New York, 1985)

St. Laurent, Cecil, *A History of Ladies' Underwear* (Michael Joseph, 1968; another version, 1975)

St. Laurent, Cecil, *A History of Women's Underwear* (Academy Editions, 1986)

Strouse, Adler Company, *The Strouse Adler Story* (New Haven, Connecticut, 1962)

Tarrant, Naomi, *Great Grandmother's Clothes: Women's Fashion in the 1880s* (The National Museums of Scotland, Edinburgh, 1986)

Taylor, Lou & Wilson, Elizabeth,

Through the Looking Glass: A History of Dress from 1860 to the Present Day (BBC Books, 1989)

Walkeley, Christina, *The Way to Wear 'em, 150 Years of Punch on Fashion* (Peter Owen, 1985)

Waugh, Norah, *Corsets and Crinolines* (Batsford, 1964; paperback, 1987)

Youll, Emily, *The History of the Corset* (1946)

Zilliacus, Benedict, *The Corset* (Oy Sjoblom Ab Finland and Ab Corsett-Industry, Sweden, 1963)

Articles

Arnold, Janet, 'Elizabethan & Jacobean Smocks & Shirts' (Waffen und Kostumkunde, 1977, Vol 12)

Mactaggart P. & R.A. 'Half a Century of Corset making: Mrs Turner's Recollections' (*Costume* No. 11, 1977)

Mactaggart P. & R.A. 'Ease, Convenience & Stays, 1750-1850' (*Costume* No. 13, 1979)

Journals and Magazines

(Bracketed dates indicate date established or volumes consulted)

La Belle Assemblée (1806-1840s); *Lady's Magazine and Monthly Museum* (1837); *The Workwoman's Guide* (1st edn. 1838, 2nd edn. 1840. Reprinted in facsimile, Bloomfield, 1975); *Punch* (est. 1841); *The Englishwoman's Domestic Magazine* (1860s); *The Queen* (est. 1861); *Harpers Bazaar* (est. 1867); *The Young Ladies' Journal* (1870s); *Sylvia's Home Journal* (1882?); *Girl's Own Paper* (1880s); *The Lady* (est. 1885); *The World of Fashion* (1890s); *Home Notes* (est. 1894); *Home Chat* (est. 1895); British *Vogue* (est. 1916); *Femina* (French 1920s-30s); *Silhouette* (French 1940s); *Tatler* (1920s); *Good Housekeeping* (1920s-50s); *Women's Journal* (1950s); *Draper's Record* (1950s); *Arena* (1980s); *Contours* (1980s); *Underlines* (1980s); *Corset and Underwear Review*, America (from 1913)

Shop Catalogues: Woollands, Harrods, Dickins & Jones (est. 1790 as Dickins Smith), George Dawson, Austin Reed, Army & Navy Stores, Marks & Spencer, Debenhams, Penberthy (est. 1883), Pryce Jones.

Mail Order Catalogues: Sears, Pryce Jones, Kays (Worcester), Damart, Next, David Nieper, Whitfords (Bury).

Patterns (dressmaking, knit, crochet): Butterick, McCalls, Bestway, Vogue, Weldons, Practical Needlework, Leachways, Simplicity.

Underwear and Corsetry Companies and Tradenames

This is a working list c1790–1990, the selection being based on the frequency of discovering advertisements, garment labels, and noting historical, literary or oral reference. For that reason it is largely British, but includes French, German and American where advertised in Britain, or represented in British museums. The list is alphabetically arranged under the best-known popular names, either company or tradename. Support industries such as shop dummies, steel busks, and dress protectors are included as appropriate.

ACHILLE SERRE: Dry cleaners, established 1870, following in the wake of Frenchman Jolly (mid-C19th), and Pullars of Perth who brought dry cleaning to Britain in 1866.

ADLIS: A London based brassière company popular from the late 1940s to the early 1950s.

ADDLEY BOURNE (Mrs): 'Family Draper, Jupon and Corset Manufacturer to the Court and Royal Family' – popular purveyor of all kinds of underwear in London of the 1860s. She manufactured corsets and crinoline frames (including in 1866 the 'Sansflectum Jupon') as well as providing drapery and trousseaux. In the 1880s she sold rational underwear.

AERTEX: Tradename of the Cellular Clothing Co. founded in 1888 by Mr Lewis Haslam, at Aldermanbury, which has a Nottingham manufactory to the present. It began by producing cellular cotton clothing, and by 1891 also produced underwear. In the 1940s it advertised 'air-conditioned' corsetry and by 1964 knitted cotton, cotton rayon and new Courtelle cotton were included. Aertex was, and still is, popular for sports and tropical wear.

ALPHA: (French) Popular in the 1930s for their rubber belt corsets.

ALPINE: Popular in the 1880s for their pure wool vests and combinations.

ALSTONS (Eastbourne): Known in the 1950s for their rubber corsets, still going in the 1980s.

AMBROSE WILSON: Mail-order corset house, from 1916 to the present.

AMERICAN BRAIDED WIRE COMPANY: Based at Shoreditch, London and known for their bustles in the 1880s. 'Braided Wire Health Bustles' made of finest watchspring silver steel wire survive in large numbers in museum collections.

ELIZABETH ARDEN: A cosmetics company to present, which began advertizing lingerie in the 1950s.

ARISTOC: Founded in 1919 as A E Allen & Co., the name Aristoc was registered in 1924, and used in advertisements from 1926. Originally the firm made fully fashioned fine-gauge silk stockings with reinforced uppers of cotton, turning to lisle ('Aristile') and rayon ('Raystoc') during WW2. From 1947 to the present Aristoc have produced nylon stockings (and tights) for both export and home markets.

ARMY & NAVY COOPERATIVE STORES: Established in London for grocery in 1871, with drapery and outfitting at its York House branch from 1879. Popular for underwear into the 1940s.

AUBADE: (French) High quality brassières and briefs to present.

AU FAIT (Foundations Ltd.): Popular for their brassières from the late 1940s. Dissolved in 1984.

BAIRNSWEAR: A long established Nottingham knitwear company, very popular for high quality woollen underwear in the 1930s. It was taken over by Courtaulds in June 1963, and continues to the present.

CHARLES BAYER (of London Wall): Popular in the 1870s as a crinoline manufacturer, he made corsets from 1879 and underclothing between 1883 and 1914. By 1891 he had a manufactory in Portsmouth and another in Bath, which was still manufacturing corsetry in the late 1970s. In 1888 he registered a chemise and a lady's belt, and in the 1890s a watch-spring corset and cycling, tennis and golfing corset. Bayer's 'CB Erect Form' corsets of c1900 borrowed from the American company Weingarten Brothers' 'erect form' design and Bayer lost the ensuing litigation. By 1930 he was manufacturing under the 'Court Royal' label.

BERLEI: An Australian corsetry company founded in 1907 by Mrs Gover and Miss Mobberley whose husband, Fred R. Burley gave the company its name (spelt Burlei) in 1919. In 1929 Berlei UK Ltd was established in Slough with showrooms in Liberty's building on Regent Street, London. During WW2 it was producing under its own label, and by the late 1940s had established factories in Wales. Berlei became part of the Courtaulds group in 1985, and in 1992 still manufactures under its own label as part of Courtaulds Textiles plc. In 1939 Berlei launched 'Undalift', from the American Under-lift brassière by the Charma Brassière Co. In 1954 the Berlei Sarong was introduced and in 1955 Sarongster. In 1960 it acquired the British rights to Teenform, and in 1962 brought out the successful Gay Slant range. Present day production

concentrates on a wide range of sizes (35 from 34A to 40FF) and speciality products such as maternity and sports bras.

BIEN JOLIE: A brand of foundation-wear manufactured by Benjamin & Johnes between 1904-30 when it was purchased by Sam Jaffe, founder of Nature's Rival. Still going in the 1960s.

BOOTH & FOX: Famous for their down petticoats of the 1860s-80s which won exhibition awards (London and Dublin).

BRAEMAR: The tradename of Innes, Henderson and Co. Ltd, who manufactured woollen knitwear in Hawick, Scotland and were popular 1930s-50s.

BRETTLE (George & Co): (Trademark 'B' in a shield with 'Oberton' underneath) Established as a haberdashers and merchants in the City of London in 1786, they opened a factory in Derby in 1803 for the manufacture of stockings. Popular for their knitwear in the 1920s-40s they were acquired by Courtaulds in 1963.

BRITISH NYLON SPINNERS (BNS): Formed by I.C.I. and Courtaulds in 1940 and producing nylon tricot slips and nightdresses in the 1950s, it was taken over by I.C.I. Fibres in 1964.

BRADLEY, VOORHIES & DAY (B.V.D.): (USA) Founded in 1876 to produce bustles, but soon diversifying into men's underwear (notably the woollen union suits with which they became synonymous). In the 1930s they made the most of new fabric technology and manufactured swimwear.

CAMP (Sam H): (USA) Began making front-lacing corsets in Jackson, Michigan c1908. Became the Goodwin Front Lace Corset Co. which by 1913 manufactured surgical supports as S H Camp and Co. Still going in the 1950s.

CANFIELD RUBBER CO: Were producing dress shields before WW1.

CAPRICE CORSETRY: A London-based label popular for their lightweight corsetry (or foundations) from the late 1940s-50s.

CARTER'S (Crinoline and Stay warehouse): Popular in London in the 1860s.

CASH AND CO (Coventry): J & J Cash Ltd produced underwear trimmings and ribbon from the mid-C19th (famous for introducing name-tags in 1889). They were still advertising lace frillings for underwear and lingerie ribbon into the 1950s.

CHARNAUX (Patent Corset Company Ltd): Founded by Dr Charnaux who patented his 'anotex' perforated rubber girdle belt in 1928 which remained popular throughout the

1930s. The company was forced to close down in 1955.

CHARNOS: Founded in 1936, producing silk and nylon stockings in the 1950s, and lingerie to the present.

CHILPRUFE: Produced top-grade woollen underclothing and was a household name from the 1920s-50s. In 1963, facing financial difficulty, it merged with Pasolds Ltd., the manufacturers of Ladybird.

CONLOWE LTD: Based in Congleton, Cheshire and popular for their knitted nylon and rayon lingerie throughout the 1950s.

CONTESSA: Founded in 1955 at Banbury, by Mr Alan Wilkie, as a shop specializing in corsetry it had established branches in Hemel Hempstead, Crawley, Stevenage, Corby and Bracknell by 1959, when it was taken over by Courtaulds Ltd. In 1991 (still under the banner of Courtaulds Textiles plc) it was a national lingerie and foundationwear retail chain with 127 branches. Bras account for over 40% of its turnover, and branded merchandise includes Berlei, Gossard, Triumph, Warner, Playtex, Charnos, Fantasie, Silhouette and Naturana.

CORAH'S: Began in 1866 as St Margaret's of Leicester manufacturing hosiery and underwear. Incorporated as Corah's plc in 1919, and soon after was approached to supply Marks & Spencer. Corah first rebuffed these advances (due to disputes over the tradename) but Marks & Spencer went on to become Corah's biggest customer. To the present.

COURTAULDS: Founded in 1816 to manufacture silk it began producing rayon in 1905. It eventually merged with British Celanese in 1957, after a period of intense rivalry, to become Britain's biggest manufacturer of viscose rayon. In 1989 the fibre and garment producing aspects split into Courtaulds plc and Courtaulds Textiles plc, the latter controlling manufacture of their various brands. In 1992 Courtaulds Textiles claim to be the biggest supplier of own-label clothing to British chain stores (Marks & Spencer represent 25% of their sales). They also claim to make more underwear than anyone in Britain under their decentralised structure which encompasses nearly 100 businesses. Brands include Gossard and Berlei for lingerie and bras, Lyle & Scott and Wolsey for knitwear, underwear and socks. Aristoc provide stockings and tights and they have also recently acquired Georges Rech, a French fashion house.

DAMART: Originated in France as a knitwear company and began in the UK as a mail order company, but is now international with over 20 UK shops. From the late 1960s it became a household name synonymous with thermal underwear, especially since the Princess of Wales announced in 1983 that she was a 'walking advertisement for Damart'.

DEBENHAMS: A London drapers and fashion shop set up as Clark & Debenham in 1813, becoming Debenham & Freebody in the mid-C19th, now an international chain of department stores. It sold hosiery, underlinen and had its own brand of corsets – in 1934 a Madame Zilva designed Debenham corsets. Amongst their popular lines was the 'English Lady' range of lingerie, launched c1960.

DICKINS AND JONES: A London department store which originated in 1790 and came under the control of Harrods in 1914. In c1900 they launched their own 'Specialite Corset' which boasted support and elegance under scientific supervision. In 1949-50 their exclusive Madeleine corset, belt and corselette range appeared.

DIM: (French) Popular in the late C20th for their high quality hosiery and lingerie.

DIOR (Christian): Christian Dior Lingerie UK was incorporated in 1973, producing quality lingerie and hosiery to the present.

DOWDING (Madame): A Corsetière of Charing Cross, whose 'Rejane', 'Royal' and cycling corsets were widely advertised in the 1890s. She also produced gentleman's belts and corsets.

DRUID: Produced registered Utility wear throughout WW2.

DU PONT de Nemours (E. I. & Co, Inc.): (USA) Their laboratories developed nylon in 1938, studies into 'polymerization' began a decade earlier. They also invented Lycra in the late 1950s.

ELLANESS: The trademark of knitwear from Hawick, Scotland, popular in the 1920s and 1930s.

ELLGEECEE (phonetic LGC): The tradename of the London Glove Company established in Cheapside in 1870, dissolved in 1984. As well as gloves it produced corsetry and underwear; camisoles, combinations and petticoats from c1900-20 survive in museum collections.

EXQUISITE FORM: (USA) Brassière company established in the UK from 1953 (to the present). Popular makes in the 1960s included Rudi-Gernreich's 'No-Bra Bra', 'No-Sides Bra', 'No-Back Bra' even a 'No-Front Bra' and corselette styled 'None-in-One'. They specialize in larger sizes, for example their 'Big Gals' range of 1990, which went up to 52″.

FANTASIE FOUNDATIONS: A Bristol-based company, catering for the fuller figure, from the late 1940s to the present. They are suppliers to Marks & Spencer, notably of bras (e.g. 1991 sports bras to E cup).

FITU: Tradename of Chappell Allen & Co., London. Popular for their corselettes and girdles in the 1930s.

FLETCHER (William Jnr.) Ltd: Based in Portsmouth, with the trademark 'WF', they produced corsets and underclothing from the 1870s, becoming an associate company of Berlei in the 1940s-50s.

FLEXEES (Artistic Foundations): (USA) Noted for their introduction of seven figure types in 1938, and popular throughout the 1940s-50s, the 'world's loveliest foundations' were designed in the USA and manufactured in the UK by 1951.

FREDERICKS OF HOLLYWOOD: Founded by Mr Frederick in 1949 to make lingerie, to the present.

GOSSARD: (USA) An international corsetry firm founded by H.W. Gossard, with UK offices established in the 1920s. Taken over by Courtaulds in 1959 it now functions within Courtaulds Textiles plc. Popular from the 1940s to the present and famous for fashion bras, notably the ever-popular 'Wonderbra', introduced in 1968.

GOSSIP: A London company popular for its lingerie of the 1950s (e.g. its 'Briar Rose' range).

HOLLYWOOD MAXWELL: (USA) Began as the Hollywood Stylist Co. in 1931 and by 1963 was operating Hollywood Vassarette, a division of Munsingwear. Berlei made a whirlpool Hollywood-Maxwell brassière in 1953.

HOM: Contemporary manufacturer of men's underwear, operating with Triumph at Swindon from 1990.

HORROCK'S, HORROCKSES: Advertising machinemade, long-cloth chemises and petticoats in London of the 1860s, by 1912 they were advertising 'Oxford' underclothing of handsewn Horrockses cloth.

IZOD: Originally named Izod & Beech, changing to Edwin Izod & Co. London, in 1864. Their trademark was an anchor, and also 'Ad Rem' was registered in 1882. Izod patented a method of steam-moulding corsets in 1868, by which he claimed 'there is no twisting of the bones or injuring the figure and by this process the shape of the corset cannot be destroyed in stitching'. Popular throughout the 1860s-70s Izod's factory in Commercial place was later taken over by the Chappell Allen Co., who ran it for a number of years.

JAEGER: The Jaeger Co. was established

by Mr L.R.S. Tomalin and his two cousins in 1883, to sell Jaeger's Sanitary Woollen Clothing – close-fitting underclothing in undyed stockinette. Their combination garments were popular with dress reformers from the 1880s onwards, but they also produced a 'Sanitary woollen corset' and in 1904 a 'bust girdle' which may be seen as a forerunner of the brassière.

JOCKEY INTERNATIONAL: Developed out of Cooper's Underwear Company (USA) making predominantly male underwear to the present.

KAYSER: Kayser-Bondor (later Kayser) underwear was popular in the 1940s, when they claimed to have existed for 35 years. Suppliers of hosiery and lingerie to Marks & Spencer, they were taken over by Courtaulds in 1964.

KESTOS: (USA) Founded by Polish-born Mrs Rosalind Klin and popular c1930-50. Famous for introducing bras with separate cups (an innovation on the 1920s bandeau) their name was synonymous with bras in the 1930s.

KEYSTONE (Knitting Mills (1928) Ltd): A Hertfordshire lingerie firm who produced Utility hosiery of the 1940s.

KLEINERT (Rubber Co, London): Manufactured dress protectors and sanitary clothing, popular 1920s-40s. For example, in 1923 they were advertising hygienic dress protector of rubber with silk or nainsook; 1937 sanitary belts, panties and knickers, and 1950 pink or white locknit knickers with fleece-nap rubber panel.

KNICKERBOX: A fast-expanding unisex underwear retail chain. Established in London in the late 1980s by 1991 they had 18 London stores, 9 branches.

KNINA, MADAME ILLA: Corsetière in Vienna and Prague, popular in the 1950s. Her clients included princesses, royal duchesses and actresses.

KOPS BROS: (USA) Corset manufacturers, established in 1894. They produced a prizewinning 'Nemo' corset in 1904, and two-way stretch corselette 'Sensation' in 1933. Kops Bros GB Ltd, claimed in 1946 to have 'made the first elastic net foundation garment ever to be used'. They marketed pantie-girdles into the 1950s under the slogan 'kitten hips for you too'.

LADYBIRD: The trademark of Pasold Ltd (manufacturers of knitted underwear since the late C19th). The Ladybird trademark was acquired in 1938 but is best-known applied to high quality children's wear from the late 1960s.

ENID LAWRENCE: Popular for brassières in the 1950s.

LAYAL: London designer of lingerie from 1986 to the present.

LEJABY: (French) Paris contemporary lingerie label, from the 1970s to the present.

LENA LASTIK: Registered underwear manufactured by Devas Routledge & Co. Ltd., Leicester. Popular from the late 1920s-50s.

LIBERTY: Tradename for corsetry produced by R. & H.W. Symington & Co. Popular from the late C19th to the 1950s – notably the child's 'liberty bodice' produced from 1908.

LILY OF FRANCE: A corset name purchased from the E.J. Weekes Co. by an American company in 1908. The Chappell Allen Co. also produced a brand named 'Lily of France' in the 1950s.

LOVEABLE BRASSIERE CO: (USA) Based in Atlanta, Georgia in the 1940s and set up in the UK c1945, taking over Pagan Ltd. of Romford, Essex. In 1940 they advertised 'the less than a dollar brassière with million dollar appeal' under the slogan 'it costs so little to look so loveable'. It sold via mail order and supplied chain stores such as Littlewoods, Woolworths, and BHS and had factories in Jamaica, Italy, Spain and Scotland before closing down in 1979.

LUCILE: The pseudonym of Lady Duff Gorden, who began making luxurious lingerie in London 1889 and was very popular to WW1.

LYLE & SCOTT: A high quality Scottish knitwear company, established in the late C19th, acquired by Wolsey in 1963, now part of Courtaulds Textiles plc. Known for their 'Y-front' male underwear since they gained the licence for 'Jockey Shorts' in 1938.

MAIDENFORM: (USA) Brassière company also producing girdles and garter belts. In the 1930s they were producing uplift 'interlude' bras with under cup stitching, and they also produced the first bra-slip. Popular throughout the 1940s and 1950s. Maiden Form (UK) Ltd. was incorporated in 1967 and survives to the present.

MARKS & SPENCER: A popular UK chainstore established in 1884 and now internationally renowned. It has many suppliers but one label – 'St Michael' which was introduced for selected goods in 1928, becoming general in 1949. Corah's were amongst their first major suppliers of underwear.

MEDIMA: (German) Leading manufacturer of high-quality thermal underwear (using angora wool) in Germany to the present.

MERIDIAN: The brand name of J.B. Lewis & Sons, a hosiery firm established in Nottingham 1893. Interlock knitwear of cotton with the texture of wool was marketed under this brand name from 1911. Meridian became the company name in 1951, which then had a range of swimwear, socks, nightwear, leisurewear and children's wear. Became part of Courtaulds Group in 1963, and part of Courtaulds Knitwear Ltd. from 1975.

MODART: (USA) Popular during the 1930s for its corsets.

MOON (Mrs Washington): Established in Regent Street in 1851 she supplied ladies' and children's underwear to the rich and famous, even to royalty.

MORLEY (I. & R. Co. Ltd.): Hosiery manufacturers established in Nottingham in 1795 (their trademark was a flying wheel). By the 1870s their sales catalogue included ladies' underlinen and corsetry of all descriptions, even chamois leather, but their name is now more generally associated with woollen undergarments. They were acquired by Courtaulds in 1968.

MY LADY: The trade name of Waterhouse Reynolds & Co. Ltd., established in Leicester in 1884, making corsets and bras popular in the 1950s.

NATURANA: A Staffordshire company making bras from the late 1950s to the present.

OKTIS: Registered in 1900 but produced corset shields, and advertised widely from the late 1890s to WW1.

PENBERTHY (Frederick): English hosier (who also sold fans and lace) established on Oxford Street in 1883.

LA PERLA: (Italian) Founded by Ada Masotti in 1954 and continuing to present. Its other trademarks include Malizia (c1983) and Occhi Verdi (1985).

PESCO: The trademark of Peter Scott & Co., a Scottish firm popular for their masculine woollen underwear since 1901. Their unisex combinations, vests and pants were popular into the 1950s.

PHILPOTT (Mr): A popular crinoline manufacturer of the 1850s-60s based in Piccadilly, London.

PLAYTEX: (USA) The brassière company, Playtex Ltd, was established in the UK in 1955 and continues into the present. Famous lines include the 'Living Girdle' of 1956 and the 'Living Bra' of the 1960s. The 'Cross your Heart' bra and the 'Eighteen Hour Girdle' appeared in the late 1960s and were supported by a huge TV advertising campaign into the 1970s, making the company a household name.

WILLIAM PRETTY & SONS: A long-established Ipswich underwear manufacturer incorporated in 1930, producing corsets and fleecy bodices for children which were popular in the

1950s. (Company dissolved in 1988).

PRETTY POLLY: Popular for their hosiery from the 1950s to the present.

PRINGLE: Scottish knitwear, from the 1930s to the present.

RECKITT & SONS Ltd: Starch manufacturers of the mid-C19th.

REGER (Janet): British designer popular since the 1970s for her luxury lingerie which retails in Europe and the USA.

RIGBY & PELLER: Renowned London retailers of up-market underwear since the 1940s and corsetières to the Queen since 1960.

ROBINSON & CLEAVER: Belfast linen drapers who opened a shop in Regent Street in 1894, specializing in hand-made Irish underlinen.

J. ROUSSEL LTD: (French) Parisian company popular from the late 1920s for their fine elastic knit 'gaine' corselette and girdle belts. In 1946 their Regent Street division offered 'belts, brassières and swimsuits, Linia belts for men' and 'Rigiflex belts for rupture'.

ROYAL WORCESTER CORSET CO: (USA) Founded in 1861 by David Hale Fanning. 'Bon Ton' was the highest grade of Royal Worcester sold in London from 1910s-20s.

SCIENTIFIC CORSETRY: Founded c1920 in West Yorkshire it catered for mature figures, manufacturing (and renovating) made-to-measure corsets and surgical corsets until 1972.

SHARP PERRIN & CO: They registered a pair of Ladies' drawers as early as 1861 but were known for their 'Rational' range of the next century. In 1902 they advertised a 'rational corset bodice' and in 1955 they were still advertising, this time 'Rational knitted vest and pantie' in wool/nylon.

SIDROY: A popular make of lingerie in the 1950s, manufactured by J. Feltz & Co. Ltd., Barry, Glamorgan.

SIEGEL & STOCKMAN: (French) Manufactured shop dummies in Paris from the 1860s, their London showroom opened c1920.

SILHOUETTE: Had its origins in Germany in 1887 but moved to Paris, and the Silhouette name in 1931. It was acquired by Spencer in 1982 and survives to the present day. Popular in the UK from the 1940s in the mid 1950s they launched 'Little X', the first brand-named two-way stretch elasticated girdle.

SOUTHALLS: A Birmingham firm manufacturing sanitary products from the late C19th to the present day, producing sanitary belts and panties in the early C20th.

SPENCER: Spencer (Banbury) Ltd. was set up in 1927, acquired Silhouette in 1982, Spirella in 1985, and is now

owned by Remploy. Known for their individually designed bespoke corsetry they once had 2,000 Spencer fitters (down to 250 in 1990). 'Rejuveno' was a popular line in the 1930s-40s (a 'Rejuveno' of the 1920s survives at Worthing). They now make surgical supports (using spiral steel stays) and post-mastectomy bras.

SPIRELLA: UK corsetry company set up in 1909 based on Marcus Merrit Beeman's invention of the spiral stay (1904) and his Spirella Company of Pennsylvania. In 1985 they were taken over by Spencer (Banbury) Ltd., and closed down in 1989.

STAPLEY & SMITH: Manufacturers and warehousemen of London Wall, whose 'S & S' trademark for corsets and corset busks was registered in 1885. They were well known for bustles from the 1870s-80s and were among the first to trademark underwear, carrying the woollen brands 'Sterling' and 'Hibernia' (the latter registered in 1889).

STROUSE, ADLER & CO: (USA) Isaac Strouse joined with Max Adler in 1866 to manufacture hoop skirts and in 1893 the company was formed.

SUNSPEL: Famous for boxer shorts, sold in UK from the late 1940s to the present.

SWAN & EDGAR: A London department store established in 1812, that went on to produce its own 'Edgar' corset.

SWANBILL: A registered brand of corset, popular from the 1870s-1900s, named after the shape of its busk. In 1891 Swanbill identified ten types of female figure and advertised different corsets accordingly.

SYMINGTONS (R. & W. H.): Corset manufacturers established in the mid-C19th, aided by the early importation of Singer sewing machines. Their most famous trademark was 'Liberty' which continued into the late C20th. They were taken over by Courtaulds in 1968.

TEENFORM: (USA) Foundation wear for teenagers, made in Britain by Berlei from 1960.

THOMSON & CO (W.S.): A US company with English and French outposts, leading crinoline manufacturers based at Cheapside, London. Their factory produced up to 4,000 crinolines daily including such registered designs as the 'Crown' (1866-8), and the 'Zepherina' or 'Winged Jupon' (a safety crinoline of 1868). Their 'glove-fitting corset' was widely advertised from the 1860s-80s, and in the 1870s they were producing 'Eiderdown corsets'.

TRES SECRETE: USA inflatable bra of the 1950s (conversely marketed in

France as 'Very Secret').

TRIUMPH INTERNATIONAL: A brassière firm which originated in Germany in 1866, registering the trademark 'Triumph' in 1902. In 1926 the first subsidiary was set up in Switzerland and in 1953 the company (Spiesshofer & Braun) assumed its present name. The British subsidiary was formed in 1954. In 1966 Triumph launched 'Doreen' one of the most popular bras for the fuller figure and one of the first to have C and D cup fittings (though by 1991 there were 51 different sizes!). Another hugely popular range was 'Sloggi', cotton and Lycra bras and briefs introduced in the 1980s. In 1991 they produced a similar 'Huggi' for Marks & Spencer, and a 'Sloggi' for men.

TWILFIT: A popular brand of foundation wear from the 1930s-50s.

VEDONIS: A household name in the 1930s for their fine rib and interlock knitwear, they produced 'Vedoknit' Utility wear during the 1940s.

VESTA: (USA) Producing corsetry between 1913 and 1963.

WARNER'S (Warner Brothers Corsets Ltd: (USA) Founded in 1874 by Dr L. G. and I. de Ver Warner (Warner Bros (UK) Ltd. incorporated 1957 is now in liquidation). They originated the 'Coraline' health corset, which sold an estimated 3/5 million pairs in 1888. Another popular line was their 1931 lastex two-way stretch corset 'Le Gant'. 'Flatterback' and 'Sta-up Top' were 1941 ranges, 'Secura' sanitary wear brief and belt range was launched in 1951, and their 'Birthday Suit' a bodyhugging pantie corselette was introduced in 1961.

WATERHOUSE REYNOLDS & Co. Ltd: A Leicester company popular in the 1950s for brassières, belts and 'My Lady' corset, bras and corselette range.

WEINGARTEN BROS: (USA) 'W.B.' had a factory in Portsmouth from 1888 manufacturing corsets which were popular in the Edwardian period, but also made foundations and bras into the 1950s.

WOLSEY: A Leicester-based knitwear company, whose high quality woollen underwear (with Cardinal's head trademark) has been renowned since the 1930s. They produced Utility wear during the 1940s (e.g. 'Brevets' 1942), and in 1967 they were acquired by Courtaulds.

W.R. WHALONIA: Tradename for corsets by William Rosenthal Whalonia registered in 1890 and popular into the Edwardian era.

Y. & N. YOUNG & NEILSON: Late C19th corsetry company of Portland Square and Norfolk Avenue Bristol, especially popular c1895-1905.

Index